Spelling
Essentials

Shireen Shuster

LONGMAN

CONTENTS

INTRODUCTION

Contents of Homework File

SECTION 1:
How to start to improve your spelling

SECTION 2:
Common spelling patterns

UNITS 25-37
cover advanced spelling patterns

UNITS 38-42
cover spelling in context

WHAT'S YOUR SPELLING LIKE?

What kind of speller are you? Do you fit any of these examples?

Katy
I think I'm a fairly good speller.
I only need help with words I've never seen before.
I don't know much about rules but after I've
written a word once, I usually remember
it the next time.

Saira
My spelling is not too bad, but
I have a few problems with difficult
endings and words that don't follow
normal rules. I use my dictionary to
check and I practise new
words.

Daniel
I'm often full of good ideas about what to
write, but my spelling lets me down so I stick to using
easy words, which can be a bit boring. I have problems
with some short words as well as longer
ones.

Are you most like Katy, Saira or Daniel? Have you ever thought of an excellent word to write – perhaps a long word – then changed your mind and used one that was easier to spell? Have you ever produced a piece of writing that you were really proud of, and then been disappointed to see lots of spelling corrections? Do you ever confuse words which sound the same but have different meanings? Are you unsure about changing words when you add new endings to them?

This book contains something to help everyone who needs to improve their spelling. We all have different spelling needs, so you will *not* find long lists of words to learn here. Instead, you will find out how to take charge of your own spelling as we show you how to tackle the words *you* need to learn.

HOW THE BOOK IS ORGANISED TO HELP YOU

The book is divided into two sections, each beginning with a list of **aims**, designed to show you the main points you will learn, and to help you to know where you are heading.

The sections are made up of **units**, each on a different spelling topic. The units also begin with an aim: what you are intended to learn from the unit. You are then introduced to the unit's key ideas, and are given practice exercises. There are three or four of these exercises per unit, which give you the practice you need to get used to the spelling pattern you are learning.

5

The exercises are often accompanied by an **Answer Page** symbol, like the one on the left here. This indicates that answers to the exercises are found in the Homework File.

 Throughout the book you will see other symbols too. Near the end of many units you will see the logo here. The letters PSD stand for **'Personal Spelling Dictionary'**. This is a reminder to look back over the words in that unit and make a note of the ones you feel you need to practise.

 The '**rule-breaker**' logo appears when you need to take special note of a few words which do not follow the spelling pattern or rule you have been learning.

In many units you will also see letters between two diagonal lines. This is a code used by many dictionaries. It indicates that you should say the *sound* of the letter or letters. For example, in the word **cartoon** the letter 'c' has the sound /k/; in the word **city** it has the sound /s/.

HOW THE HOMEWORK FILE FITS IN

This Student's Book is accompanied by a **Homework File**. For each unit in the Student's Book, there is at least one photocopiable sheet in the Homework File (called a **Copymaster**). The copymaster is designed to give you more practice at home, to help you to really fix the spelling rules and patterns in your head.

CONCLUSION

This book will not teach you every word you need to know – but it will teach you many hundreds of words and give you the skills to learn to spell many more. Its systematic, step-by-step approach takes you through all the major spelling patterns, and shows you that spelling is much more logical than we might sometimes think.

At the end of the course you will have the confidence to have a go at spelling any word you want to use – and the chances are that you will get it right!

SHIREEN SHUSTER

How to start to improve your spelling

AIMS:

★ to help you organise your spelling practice in a way that suits your needs

★ to find out effective ways of learning spellings

★ to learn some background information on the structure of words

In this section you will:

★ start a 'Personal Spelling Dictionary' to record and practise words

★ explore how we use several different senses to learn spellings

★ find out how to use memory tricks to help with confusing words

★ look closely at vowels, consonants and syllables

★ learn about the rules to follow when adding endings to words.

Remember:

★ the Homework File has activity sheets to give you extra practice

★ the Homework File also has answers to some of the exercises in the units

★ there is a self-assessment test at the end of the section, so you can chart your progress.

1 Start to improve your spelling

Aim:
to discover how *you* can improve your own spelling

A WHAT KIND OF SPELLER ARE YOU?

1 Think about your spelling needs.

★ Have you always found spelling fairly easy or is it a problem for you?
★ What sort of comments have teachers made about your written work?
★ Which words do you find difficult?
★ How do you remember new words?
★ Do you think correct spelling is important? How important? Why?
★ What sort of help do you think you need?

Write a paragraph with the title '**Spelling: My Views**'.

2 Compare your views with a friend. You will probably find several differences. One person has different spellings needs from another, so organise your learning in a way that helps *you*.

B ORGANISING YOUR LEARNING

Concentrate on the words which *you* find a problem. The first step is to start your own **Personal Spelling Dictionary**.

It will have three main uses:

1 Keep a note of spellings to learn

These might be corrections from a piece of work, new words from this book or new words you wish to use yourself.

Make <u>absolutely sure</u> you have the <u>correct</u> spelling written down. Either look in a dictionary or ask an adult – a parent or a teacher – to check it.

2 Learn spellings

Use the 'Study, Cover, Write, Check' method. These are the steps to follow:

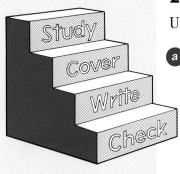

a STUDY each word carefully.

★ Can you split it into smaller parts?
★ Do the sounds in the word help you?
★ Is there anything about its spelling which is similar to other words you know?

★ Is there anything unusual about its spelling?

★ Say the word aloud and spell it using the letter names.

b COVER the word and ...

c WRITE it from memory.

★ This will fix it in your mind more firmly than if you just copy it.

d CHECK to see if you were right.

★ If yes – write it twice more, covering the word each time.

e If you were wrong, go back to the first step and study the word again.

3 Test yourself – in three steps

a When you have learnt a new word, write it at the <u>back</u> of your 'Personal Spelling Dictionary', with the heading '**Targets for Testing**'.

b Once a week, ask someone to test you on all the words you have learnt.

c Keep a record of your scores, tick off the words you are sure you know, and make a note of any which need more practice.

As you work through this book you will see this symbol at the end of many units. It reminds you to look back at your work and put any difficult words in your Personal Spelling Dictionary.

Follow-on: Start your own Personal Spelling Dictionary **NOW**. Look through your recent English work to see which spellings to include.

If you are already a good speller and have made very few mistakes recently, try out the system with these difficult words:

★ definitely   Mediterranean   embarrassed   moustache   rhinoceros

Key point – Keep a record of the words you need to learn.

COPYMASTER 1 A/B

2 Use your senses

Aim:
to understand how using your senses can help
improve your spelling

A | WHICH SENSES?

How many of the five senses do you think you use when you are learning
how to spell new words?

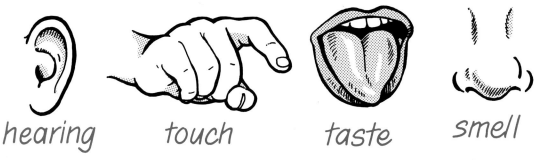

sight   hearing   touch   taste   smell

The answer is, you use hearing and sight – and touch too.

B | HEARING

We use our *sense of hearing* to spell words we may never have seen. Say the
word, listen to the sounds inside it and write the letters which say those
sounds.

These are names of characters in a computer game. Even though you have
not seen them before, you can read them from the sounds of the letters.

★ Zool   Flarm   Dreckle   Quilp

1 Work with a partner. Take it in turns to make up new names for a character
   in a computer game about aliens. Write down the names and then see if you
   have both spelt them the same way.
2 Is there more than one way of spelling the same sound?

C | SIGHT

You use your *sense of sight* to spell well. Every time you read a word, a picture
of it forms in your brain, like a photograph. You can tell if your spelling *looks*
right because you know what it looked like in print.

Look at these three tries at the same word. Which *looks* right?

★ frend   friend   freind

Try with these words. Write down the correct one from each line.

1. elephant   ellephunt   elefant
2. withe   with   whith
3. pictur   picture   picher
4. bilding   building   billding
5. world   werld   wirld

The more you read, the more your brain will form pictures of correct spelling patterns.

D | TOUCH

The *sense of touch*, or feeling, is an important part of spelling.

1. Write your name with your eyes closed.

You did it without looking and without thinking about what it sounds like. This is because you have written it so many times that your hand works like a robot. You do the same thing with other words that you know very well and with the letter patterns that are in many words.

2. Which letter pattern comes in all these words?

★ **jumping**   **swing**   **swimming**   **writing**   **fling**

Write **'ing'** with your eyes closed. Use *joined-up* writing – '**cursive**'– as this will help your hand to work automatically.

3. Spot the letter pattern in each set of words and write that pattern with your eyes closed. Use cursive writing.

danger   strap   apple
driver   string   people
rider   struck   topple

> **Key point** – Use your senses of sound, sight and even touch to improve your spelling.

3 Memory tricks for spelling

Aim:
to find different ways of remembering difficult words

A · HELP YOUR MEMORY

Most of us have a few words which we always spell wrongly. Invent your own special *memory tricks* for these words.

A memory aid is called a **mnemonic** (pronounced 'nemonic').

B · DIFFERENT KINDS OF MEMORY TRICKS

A sentence

You might have learnt to spell '**because**' by repeating a sentence where each word begins with the letters of '**because**':

Babies **E**at **C**ustard **A**nd **U**ncle **S**ucks **E**ggs.

Imagine you are helping a young child with spelling. Quite often the word '**goes**' is wrongly spelt. (Some people spell it 'gose'.) Work in small groups and make up a sentence mnemonic for 'goes'.

Pictures and crosswords

Words which sound the same but are spelt differently can cause a problem, for example:

★ leek   leak

Which one is the vegetable and which is something, perhaps water, escaping?

A drawing often helps to fix a fact in the memory. The '**A**' in **LEAK** and the '**A**' in **TAP** helps you remember which way to spell the word that means water escaping.

Use this 'crossword' method for several other spellings. For example:

★ To remember there's an 'a' in **metal**, link it with a tin **can** (of beans?).
★ To remember there's an 'h' in **character**, link it with **hero**.

Make a crossword mnemonic for either 'metal' or 'character'. Include some drawing in your mnemonic.

Letter pattern links

Make a link between the word you are trying to learn and a word you know which contains the same spelling pattern.

Example:

Alan has a problem with **guitar**. He forgets to put '**u**' before '**i**'. As Alan knows that the word **fruit** has the letter pattern '**ui**', he remembers 'The guy with the g**ui**tar drinks fr**ui**t j**ui**ce'.

1 The '**ie**' in **believe** can cause problems. Write a sentence to link 'believe' with another 'ie' word (for example: **thief**, **field**, **chief**, **pie**).

2 Now do the same for the word **mystery**.

Words within words

Look inside a word for small words you recognise, for example:

★ 'An **island** **is** land surrounded by water.'

3 Write the word **Parliament**. Find the man's name inside it and underline it.

4 Write **terrible**. Find a three-letter word inside it and underline it.

5 Write **height**. Find another word inside it and underline it.

Often the best mnemonics are the ones you make up yourself. Tom kept confusing **steel** (the metal) and **steal** (to rob). He knew **steel** is a <u>strong</u> metal so he invented the mnemonic '<u>Two E's</u> are <u>stronger</u> than one'. This is a good mnemonic because:

★ it is short, simple and 'snappy', and easy to remember

★ it means something to the person who invented it.

Follow-on: Which words have *you* found hard to remember? Use the ideas for mnemonics and make up some of your own. Add them to your PSD.

> **Key point –** The best mnemonics are short, simple, funny – and personal to you.

4 Vowels and consonants

Aim:
to look at how words are made up of vowels and consonants

A   VOWEL AND CONSONANT SOUNDS

Sounds in words give us many clues about spelling.

The sounds which make up words can be split into two different groups, **vowels** and **consonants**.

These are the five vowels: **A   E   I   O   U**

Does that mean all the other letters of the alphabet are consonants?
Yes and no! Which letter comes in each of the following words?

★ Try my cherry yoghurt today.

The letter '**y**' can be a vowel or a consonant, depending on the sounds it makes.

★ In **yoghurt** it has a consonant sound.
★ In **try** and **my** it sounds like '**i**', therefore it is a vowel.
★ In **cherry** it sounds like '**e**', therefore it is a vowel.
★ Sometimes it joins with another vowel as part of its sound, as in **d<u>ay</u>**, **b<u>oy</u>**, **monk<u>ey</u>**.

Count the vowels and consonants in the following sentence. Write down how many there are of each.

★ The crash was caused by driving too fast on icy roads.

B   DO ALL WORDS NEED BOTH VOWELS AND CONSONANTS?

1 The names of these alien creatures are written in their own language, which is nothing like English. Try to pronounce the names.

kbnr   hrbsv   pfgd

Did you find that an easy task? Why not? What is missing?

2 Now read these alien names:

★ ueeo   aioe   auea

What is missing this time? Are they any easier to say than the first set? Vowels have stronger sounds than consonants, so they can be pronounced on their own.

3 Look at the five vowels again:

★ a   e   i   o   u

Some of them even make a word just as they are. Which ones?

4 Consonants cannot make words on their own. They have to be <u>with</u> vowel sounds to make any sense. The following 'words' cannot be pronounced, but they would make real words if we put the missing vowels back.

★ schl   grdn   sstr   snk   ftbll   cmptr

Hunt the missing vowels. Work out what they are, then write the full words. (You may be able to think of more than one answer for some words.)

5 Try all the vowels in turn in each of the following spaces. If it makes a real word, write it. Make as many words as you can.

★ st-p   b-ll   s-ng   ch-p   r-g   m-st   l-ck

Read the clues below, then fill in the missing consonants. Warning: missing consonant puzzles can be quite hard! Why do you think this is so?

6 kind of transport ae-o--a-e
7 large animal -i--o-o-a-u-
8 planet -u-i-e-

9 board game -o-o-o-y
10 school subject -i--o-y
11 flower -a--o-i-

> **Key point –** Most words contain at least one vowel and one consonant.

5 Vowel sounds

Aim:
to identify long and short vowel sounds

A VOWELS AND THEIR SOUNDS

Most people find it quite easy to spell consonant sounds. However, vowel sounds can be far more troublesome, so they need extra care.

Read this sentence:

★ Sam asks how many yachts are sailing along the Channel today.

1 Which vowel occurs most in the sentence?
2 Cover up the starred sentences on this page, then carefully pronounce each word that contains that vowel.
3 How many **different** sounds can you find for that one vowel?

Did you spot all of these?

★ The 'a' in **Sam** and **Channel** has the sound /a/ as in **actor**.
★ The 'a' in **sailing** and **today** has the sound /a/ as in **alien**.
★ The 'a' in **many** has the sound /e/ as in **exam**.
★ The 'a' in **yachts** has the sound /o/ as in **octopus**.
★ The 'a' in **are** has the sound /ar/ as in **artist**.
★ The 'a' in **asks** can be pronounced /a/ as in **actor** or /ar/ as in **artist**, depending on your accent. Which do you say? In which part of the country is it pronounced the other way?
★ The 'a' in **along** has a very weak sound, a bit like /u/ in **upset**.

Now do the same for the following sentence. Read it, listening carefully to the vowel sounds.

★ Rob the hopeless pilot has lost his aeroplane and wonders who has stolen it.

Make a note of all the different sounds you can find for the vowel 'o', and compare your notes with a friend.

The same vowel can be used to spell several different sounds. One of the most important things to learn about them is the difference between the *long* and *short* vowel sounds.

B LONG VOWEL SOUNDS

Long vowel sounds are the same as the *names* of the letters.

16

1 Say these words and listen for the long vowel sound.

a	<u>a</u>lien	tod<u>ay</u>	<u>age</u>
e	evening	equal	zero
i	dive	item	bright
o	broke	ozone	follow
u	use	universe	fortune

y has the long /i/ sound in words like:

cry   shy   supply

2 Say them again, keeping each long vowel sound going for about two seconds.

Some dictionaries use a special code to show how to pronounce vowel sounds. Long vowels are often marked with a line above them, called a **macron**:

★ dānger   mēdium   fīnal   bōnus   tūna

Write the words from question one and mark each long sound with a macron.

C   SHORT VOWEL SOUNDS

The *short vowel sounds* are:

/a/ for **ant**   /e/ for **egg**   /i/ for **ill**   /o/ for **odd**   /u/ for **under**

Some dictionaries put a curly mark above the short vowels. This is called a **breve**:

★ ăpple   chĕrry   fĭg   ŏrange   plŭm

Read each pair of words below and decide which one has the short vowel sound. Write the word and mark the short vowel with a breve.

a hamster, whale   **e** eagle, ferret   **i** tiger, mink   **o** dolphin, goat
u skunk, unicorn

> **Key point –** The same vowel can be used to spell several different sounds.

6 Short vowel sounds

Aim:
to look at different ways of spelling short vowel sounds

A FINDING SHORT VOWEL SOUNDS

The short vowels sounds are: **ǎ** as in 'z**a**p', **ě** as in 'y**e**t', **ǐ** as in 'l**i**p', **ǒ** as in 'f**o**g', and **ǔ** as in 'm**u**m'.

1 Write these words and mark the short vowels with a breve.

★ Jan Jen Jim John Bud

2 Write these words. Decide which of the vowels are short and mark them with a breve.

★ sparrow robin blackbird moorhen seagull

3 Fill each of the gaps with one short vowel to make a word.

★ -nside -bject -ttic br-sh ind-x

4 You can fill each of these five gaps with different short vowels to make different words. How many words can you make altogether?

★ b-d s-ng b-g fl-sh l-mp

Score: 12 or above, good; 15 or above, excellent.

B WAYS OF SPELLING SHORT VOWEL SOUNDS

Short vowel sounds are usually quite simple to spell. Most of the time you need just one letter. But *BEWARE!* There are a few traps.

Look at these words and spot how the vowel sound is spelt in each case:

red but *dead*   **bed** but *head*
mist but *mystery*   **Jim** but *gym*
on but *swan*   **rod** but *squad*
nutty but *nothing* **bubble** but *trouble*

Write out these sentences, filling in the gaps.

1 In **heaven** the /ě/ sound is spelt with two letters, _ and _ .
2 In **crystal** the /ǐ/ sound is spelt with the letter _ .
3 In **want** the /ǒ/ sound is spelt with the letter _ .

④ In **Monday** the /ŭ/ sound is spelt with the letter _ .

⑤ In **touch** the /ŭ/ sound is spelt with two letters, _ and _ .

C | SPOTTING ODDLY-SPELT SHORT VOWEL SOUNDS

① Write out the five vowels, one on each line. Put a breve above each to show it is a short vowel sound. Read these words aloud and listen to the vowel sound in each word. Write the word on the correct line for that sound.

> ★   **love**   **wash**   **deaf**   **hymn**   **young**   **squash**   **bread**   **myth**

② Find the words which rhyme. Write out the words, putting the rhyming pairs together. The first pair is put together for you.

> ★   <u>**done**</u>   **spot**   **heaven**   **Egypt**   **stung**
> ★   <u>**stun**</u>   **seven**   **young**   **what**   **slipped**

Remember: If you are unsure about any of the words in this unit, put them in your Personal Spelling Dictionary.

Follow-on: Look in any book and practise spotting different ways of spelling the short vowel sounds.

> **Key point –** Listening to sounds will help you to spell. But it is not enough. To be sure you are right, you must also remember the tricky words.

7 Long vowel sounds

Aim:
to look at different ways of spelling long vowel sounds

A REVISION

Can you remember which vowel sounds are called *long* vowels?

Write the following words. Listen to the *first* vowel sound in each word and mark it with:

★ a breve for a short vowel, or
★ a macron for a long vowel.

1. athletics, racing,
2. hockey, rowing,
3. chess, speedway,
4. rugby, scuba-diving
5. fishing, riding,

B MAKING LONG VOWEL SOUNDS

In Unit 6 you saw that short vowels are usually spelt with just one letter. Long vowels often need a helping hand from other letters.

★ Sometimes you need to add 'e' after the next consonant: **cap > cape**
★ Sometimes you need to add another vowel: **ran > rain**
★ Sometimes that extra vowel is 'y': **stay**
★ Sometimes extra consonants are needed: **grow, sight**

1. Look at all these different ways of spelling the long vowel sounds. What sound can you hear on each line? Which extra letters have been added to make the vowel long? Write the words and circle the extra letter.

a. make stain play
b. these sweep clean chief honey
c. swipe night tie
d. rope boast shadow toe
e. tune rescue

2. Now try these. Add extra letters to make real words with long vowel sounds. Write the words.

a. hat- cla-m ma-
b. them- ste-p le-p
c. rip- si- -t di-
d. not- co-t arro-
e. tub- cu-

20

C | USE YOUR EYES

Remember to *use your eyes* to see which long vowel *looks* right.

Read the clues and write the correct word.

1. It's wet — **rane / rain**
2. Sit on it — **seat / seet**
3. Opposite of wet — **dry / drie**
4. Wash with it — **sope / soap**
5. Riches — **fortune / fortewn**

D | RHYMES

Words which rhyme will not always have the same vowel spelling. For example:

★ **feel, seal   toe, arrow   few, value**

Write as many words as you can to rhyme with each of the four words below. How will you know if you have spelt them correctly?

1. **tail**   2. **bean**   3. **night**   4. **hole**

E | ODD LONG VOWEL SOUNDS

A few words use odd letters to spell their long vowel sounds. These words have the long sound /ā/:

★ **great** (meaning 'large')   **break** (meaning 'gap' / 'smash')   **steak** (the meat)

These words have the long /ū/ sound. What is odd about their spelling?

★ **few   stew   new   dew** (dampness)

Practise these words by writing one sentence for each word.

> **Key point –** There are many ways to spell the long vowel sounds. Take care to make the right choice.

8 Words which sound the same

Aim:
to look at words which sound exactly the same but don't mean the same thing

A | HOMOPHONES

How do you spell the name of this insect? Is it a **beetle** or a **beatle**? Take a vote in class and see if you all agree.

Many people confuse these two spellings because the words sound exactly the same. Words which sound the same but have a different meaning are called **homophones**.

The word 'homophone' comes from two Greek words: *homos* meaning 'same' and *phone* meaning 'sound'.

A C T I V I T Y

There are 11 pairs of homophones all mixed up here. Write each one next to its partner.

1. **wait** w _____
2. **steel** st _____

wait	steel	been
road	site	grown
due	break	so
cheap	groan	sight
dew	sail	brake
cheep	weight	bean
sew	steal	rode	sale

B | HOW TO LEARN HOMOPHONES

In Unit 2 you read that listening to sounds is important in spelling. But if two different words sound exactly the same, your sense of hearing is not much help to you. Remember the other methods you know:

★ Use your eyes. Write down the possible spellings and see which looks right.

Which is wet, **rain** or **rein**?

★ If you are still unsure, check in a dictionary to see which word has the meaning you want:

night: the dark time between evening and morning
knight: a nobleman of the Middle Ages

22

★ If it's hard to remember, make up a mnemonic. The best mnemonics for homophones are those which give you a clue about the meaning:

'B*ee*s and b*ee*tles are insects.
The B*ea*tles played music with a b*ea*t. (That's how they got their name.)'

C | WRITE THE RIGHT WORD

Write each sentence choosing the correct words. How will you check if you are unsure?

1. It's **bean/been** a **week/weak** since I had **beans/beens** for **tea/tee**.
2. A **great/grate** big **beach/beech** tree has **groan/grown** by the **road/rode**.
3. He **waits/weights** for the **plain/plane** which he **nose/knows** is **due/dew** to land at **eight/ate** o'clock.

D | WHICH WORD IS WHICH?

Read the clues and find the correct words. Write them next to each other.

toe   mane
queue sight
site   cue
main   brake
feat   break
tow   feet

1. hair on a horse's neck
2. put socks on these
3. snap or smash
4. five of these on each foot
5. a place to build
6. a line of people
7. most important
8. an act of strength or courage
9. stop the car
10. pull along
11. something to see
12. a stick used in snooker

Follow-on: Look back at your work and think which words you were unsure of. Put these words in your Personal Spelling Dictionary. How are you going to remember them? Make up some mnemonics to help with the hardest ones.

> **Key point –** Homophones need extra care. Check them in a dictionary if you are unsure. Make a point of learning any problem ones.

9 Long words and syllables

Aim:
to see how splitting long words into syllables can help your spelling

A | WHAT ARE SYLLABLES?

Which of these sentences is the most interesting start to a story?

★ The girl went down the path.

★ Elizabeth struggled desperately along the gloomy, mud-spattered path.

Longer words can be harder to spell. Don't fall into the trap of being boring by only using short words. If you want to use a long word, make it easier to spell by breaking it down into smaller parts, called **syllables**.

A syllable is a beat in a word. Look at this tune:

Hap-py Birth-day to you!

To sing the word **happy** we need *two* notes - one for '**hap**' and one for '**py**'.
To sing the word **birthday** we need *two* notes - one for '**birth**' one for '**day**'.
'Happy' and 'birthday' each have two *syllables*.
How many syllables are there in **to** and **you**?

1 You can tell how many syllables are in a word by tapping out its beat. Use one finger to tap out the beat of these words:

★ **reptile   crocodile   snake   alligator   turtle   rattlesnake**

2 In your book make three columns with these headings:

ONE SYLLABLE	TWO SYLLABLES	THREE SYLLABLES

Count the number of syllables in each of the following words and write the word in the correct column.

★ **taxi   bus   lorry   train   transporter   bicycle   ferry   aeroplane
ambulance   coach   submarine   liner   truck**

24

B USING SYLLABLES TO HELP YOUR SPELLING

When you want to spell a longer word, break it up into syllables and write each one in turn. The rule is: <u>each syllable must contain a vowel sound.</u>

1 Notice how the following words have been split so that there is a vowel sound in each syllable. Write them and underline each vowel. The first one has been done for you.

★ d<u>e</u>n-t<u>i</u>st   ty-pist   brick-lay-er   dri-ver   car-pen-ter   ac-tor

Watch out! If two vowels together will make just one sound, they belong in the same syllable:

★ t<u>ea</u>-cher   w<u>ai</u>t-er   c<u>ou</u>n-try

Sometimes a vowel is silent, so it does not make another syllable:

★ mis-tak<u>e</u>   com-plet<u>e</u>   in-sid<u>e</u>

Sometimes a vowel on its own can be a syllable:

★ <u>u</u>-ni-form   <u>i</u>-de-<u>a</u>   vid-<u>e</u>-<u>o</u>

2 Write these words, splitting them into syllables. Pronounce them carefully to make sure you get the correct number of syllables.

Liverpool: *Liv-er-pool*	Manchester	London
Scotland	Yorkshire	Northumberland
America	Germany	Australia

C SOME UNUSUAL WORDS

Put the words **Io** and **straight** in your Personal Spelling Dictionary.

'Io' is the name of one of the moons around the planet Jupiter. Do you think 'Io' is the shortest two-syllable word in English? Is it possible to find a shorter one? Can you think of a longer one-syllable word than 'straight'?

> **Key point** – Long words are easier to spell if you split them into syllables.

10 Introducing suffixes

Aim:
to see how suffixes change words

A | ROOT WORDS AND THEIR SHOOTS

You can make some words longer and change their meaning by adding bits to the end. Look at this example:

★ SHARP ➤ sharp<u>er</u> sharp<u>est</u> sharp<u>en</u> sharp<u>ened</u> sharp<u>ener</u>

The endings are called **suffixes.** Each word in this box has a suffix:

| shouting   played   silently   toaster   sweetest   golden |
| cupful   lucky   useless   darkness   faxes   lightish   enjoyment |

Under the following three headings write the words above in full, then split them into the root word and the suffix. For example:

WHOLE WORD	ROOT WORD	SUFFIX
jumped	jump	ed

B | BE CAREFUL WITH '-FUL'

Look at the spelling of these words:

★ cheerful   restful   painful   helpful   wonderful   disgraceful

The suffix '**ful**' means 'full of' but it only needs *one* letter '**l**'. Remember it this way:

★ A word with a suffix is long enough already without needing two 'l's.

Add the suffix 'ful' to these root words. Write the new word.

★ fear   mug   power   delight   plate   forget   tune   boast

C PROOFREADING

Several suffixes have been left out of this letter. Proofread it carefully and write it out, adding the correct suffixes.

> Dear Sir,
> Although I enjoy watch film about space travel I do think it is very waste to spend money try to contact other planet. We could never real travel out of this galaxy so it is use to pretend we could. There are plenty of project at home which are in much great need of money, for example, school and hospital. I would be interest to know how many reader are in agree with me.
> Yours sincere
> Liam Baxter (aged 13)

D VOWEL AND CONSONANT SUFFIXES

cooking	hunted	dampish
hopeless	buses	eats
sadness	brighter	thicken
spoonful	kindly	crafty

1 Write out the words in the box and highlight or underline the suffixes. Each of the 12 words has a different suffix.

2 Divide the suffixes into two groups:
★ suffixes that begin with a vowel
★ suffixes that begin with a consonant.

Remember that 'y' in a word like **lucky** has a *vowel sound*, so it counts as a *vowel suffix*. Write the suffixes under the headings:

VOWEL SUFFIXES	CONSONANT SUFFIXES
ing	ly
....	......

Follow-on: Look in any book for words with different suffixes. Split the words and write them like this: **sharp + er = sharper**

Key point – Notice whether a suffix begins with a vowel or a consonant.

11 Suffixes: When to double a letter

Aim:
to find out why we sometimes have to double a letter when we add a suffix

---

A | VOWEL AND CONSONANT PATTERNS

You already know that one way to spell a long vowel sound is to put the letter '**e**' after the end consonant (e.g. hat ➔ hate). If a word has a 'vowel-consonant-vowel' pattern, the first vowel is usually a long sound. Write these words and mark the v-c-v pattern, as in the first example:

v c v
final   zero   music   lazy   local

Look at the following words. Some have suffixes but some are just complete words. They all have two syllables and two vowels. Some have only one consonant between the vowels, but some have two consonants separating the vowels.

1. super supper
2. broken shocking
3. matter later
4. dinner diner
5. Peter better
6. robot robber
7. baking backing
8. runner unit
9. pilot pillow

Put the following two headings in your book and sort the words above into two groups. The first pair are done for you:

ONE CONSONANT BETWEEN THE VOWELS	TWO CONSONANTS BETWEEN THE VOWELS
super	supper

Read all the words in each list. Listen carefully to the first vowel sound in each word. What do you notice? Can you see and hear a pattern? Do you agree with these two statements?

★ In the words with one consonant between the vowels, the first vowel is long.

★ In the words with two consonants between the vowels, the first vowel is short.

Check that your lists match this pattern. Then mark the first vowel in each word, using the code you know: a macron (¯) for a long vowel and a breve (˘) for a short vowel.

B ADDING VOWEL SUFFIXES TO WORDS

Read these pairs of words and look at the spelling patterns:

★ **hoping, hopping   taping, tapping**

Which pattern gives you a long vowel? Which pattern gives you a short vowel?

The rule is:

When you add a vowel suffix to a word with a short vowel sound, you must double the final letter of the root word. This protects the short vowel from 'attack'.

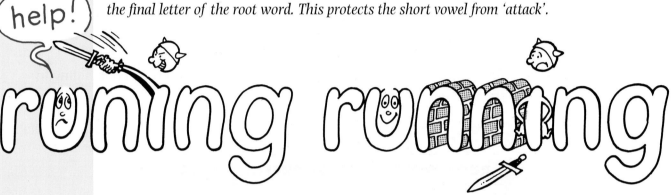

The second vowel is like an invader who is trying to attack the first vowel and make it change its way of life. If the invader gets close enough, the first vowel will be forced to say its long sound, /ū/. But, in the next picture there is a strong wall of two consonants to protect the first vowel so the invader can't attack. The first vowel can now carry on as before, with its short sound /ŭ/ which, of course, will make the word **running**.

Put three headings in your book. Add the suffix '**ing**' to these root words:

★ **hop   skip   ban   thud   pot   grin   flap   bat   wet**

ROOT WORD		ADD THE VOWEL SUFFIX		RESULT
hop	+	ing	=	hopping

Key point – When you add a vowel suffix to a root word which ends with a short vowel and only one consonant, you must double that consonant to protect the vowel from attack.

12 Suffixes: Double or not?

Aim:
to practise doubling consonants – and to know when you don't need to double them

A MORE VOWEL SUFFIXES

You have practised the doubling rule with the suffix '**ing**'. Follow the same rule with all the vowel suffixes. Remember: if a suffix begins with a vowel, it will attack a short vowel sound and make it say its long sound – unless you build up the defences.

Read these examples. Then copy the table below into your book, filling in the final column.

★ rob – robber   slip – slipped   flat – flatten   sun – sunny   red – reddish

ROOT WORD	VOWEL SUFFIX	RESULT
red	en	
bat	ed	
shop	er	
flat	est	

B DON'T OVERDO IT

You now know *when* to double and *why* you are doing it. So don't fall into the trap of doubling when you should not do so.

1 Can you see why there is no need to double the final consonant in these examples?

★ help + ing   land + ed   camp + er   damp + en

Write the words and write a sentence explaining clearly why you did not need to double anything.

2 Some suffixes start with a consonant:

★ mad + ly   sad + ness   cup + ful   hat + less

Can you see why there is no need to double the final consonant? Write out the words and then write a sentence explaining clearly why you did not need to double anything.

Copy the following table into your book and complete it. Decide whether or not you need to double the final consonant, put a tick in the correct column and write the whole word.

ROOT WORD	SUFFIX	JUST ADD	DOUBLE	RESULT
tip	ed		✔	tipped
pot	ful	✔		potful
bad	ness			
flat	est			
slop	y			
jot	er			
risk	ed			

C A FINAL LOOK

Look back at the 'invader' mnemonic in Unit 11. Only the *short* vowels need strong protection from attack. Read these words:

★ cleanest stayed hoaxer rainy oiling shouted

None of them have short vowel sounds, so they do not need any extra defences. Try this final 'mixed bag' of words. For each one, ask yourself these two questions:

★ Is there a short vowel that needs protection?
★ Is there already a defensive wall of two consonants?

ROOT WORD	SUFFIX	JUST ADD	DOUBLE	RESULT
scream	ed	✔		screamed
room	ful			
hid	en			
bump	er			
deep	est			
skin	y			

Key point – Check carefully to see when you have to double a letter.

Section 1: Self-assessment page

Complete this page to see how much you have learnt in Section One.

1 Write out these instructions, filling in the gaps.

To learn a spelling, do not just copy the word. Do this instead:

- STUDY the word carefully.
- ___ it up and write it from ___
- ___ to see if you were ___

2 Read these words and listen for the sound of the first vowel:

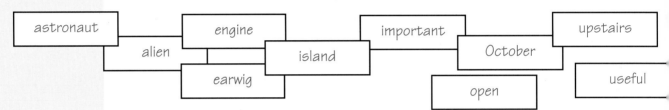

astronaut		engine		important		upstairs
alien			island		October	
	earwig				open	useful

Now sort the words and write them in two sets:

a) Words which begin with a *short* vowel.
b) Words which begin with a *long* vowel.

3 Write out this spelling rule, filling in the gaps:

If you want to add a vowel suffix to a root ___ which ends with one short vowel and one consonant, you must ___ the last consonant. If you don't do this, the vowel in the ___ word will have a ___ sound.

4 Proofread this paragraph and write it out correctly. There are 12 mistakes:

On the hotest day of last summer we went swiming in the river. My skiny friend steped on some slime-covered rocks which were hiden under the surface. He skided across the rocks, yeling for help. As he fell he bumped his bottom on some jaged rocks and ended up a lot weter than he intended. We all thought it was quite funy and that made him even mader.

5 Answer these questions in sentences:

a) How many words have you put in your Personal Spelling Dictionary?
b) Have they come just from your English lessons or from other sources also?
c) Have you arranged any tests for these words?
d) Do you think your PSD is helping to improve your spelling?

Common spelling patterns

AIMS:

★ to improve your spelling further by looking at common but often misspelt words

★ to develop your interest in spelling by looking at words in a wider context

★ to continue building up your own Personal Spelling Dictionary

In this section you will:

★ learn more about adding suffixes to root words

★ find out how to tackle words with weak vowel sounds which give you no clue about their spelling

★ explore how to make best use of dictionaries and computer spell-checks

★ find out how English spelling developed – and how it is still changing in the modern world

Remember:

★ keep adding to your Personal Spelling Dictionary, including words not in this book that you also need to learn

★ use the activity sheets in the Homework File to reinforce what you have learnt in class

★ check your answers to some of the exercises in the units by looking in the Homework File.

13 'Wa', 'war' and 'wor' words

Aim:
to look at words containing 'wa', 'war' and 'wor'

A THE WILD WAYS OF 'W'

The letter 'w' has a wicked way of bewitching vowel sounds. The sound /wŏ/, is often spelt 'wa'.

Read these words:

★ **was want what wander Wally wash wallet watch swan swamp**

Write the following sentences, choosing from 'o' or 'a' to spell the missing /ŏ/ sound correctly.

1 B-b w-s stung by a w-sp.
2 W-tch where you w-nder. You don't w-nt to fall in a sw-mp.
3 T-mmy loves w-tching the sw-ns from the river bank.
4 W-lly likes w-tching the ducks w-ddling by the p-nd.
5 D-n l-st his w-tch and w-llet when he w-s r-bbed in the w-shroom.

Here are three rule-breakers. Write them down.

★ **wobble   wonky   wok**

B WARNING – LOOK OUT FOR 'WAR'!

After 'w' the /or/ sound is spelt 'ar'.

Write out the clues, then choose correct 'war' words to fill the blank spaces.

★ **war   warm   ward   wart   swarm   dwarf**
   wardrobe   warden   warble   swarthy

1 Quite hot. _____
2 Bird song. _____
3 Clothes cupboard. _____
4 Conflict. _____
5 Fairy-tale character. _____
6 Hospital room. _____
7 Bees in flight. _____
8 Person in charge. _____
9 Growth on the skin. _____
10 Dark-skinned. _____

Watch out for this rule-breaker:

★ You look **worn** out.
★ Why have you **worn** that awful old sweater?

34

C 'WOR' FOR /WER/

You know how to spell **were** – but look at these other words with the sound /wer/:

★ word work worm world worse worst worship worth worthy

After '**w**' the /er/ sound is usually spelt '**or**'.

1 A 'compound word' is made from two other words joined together. Choose a 'wor' word to complete these compound words:

★ _____bench   _____while   book_____   _____search

2 Choose a 'wor' word to complete these phrases:

★ _____ wonders / for what it's _____ / _____ of mouth / if the _____ comes to the _____ / best of both _____

D WORK IT OUT!

Find the word that is wrongly spelt in each of these sentences and write it correctly.

1 Your illness will get worse if you don't swollow this.
2 Millions were killed in two werld wars.
3 Bees can swarm with no worning.
4 My werst job is tidying my wardrobe.
5 Nobody wants that werthless old paper.

Follow-on: Look in a dictionary for some more example of 'wa', 'war' and 'wor' words.

Key point – Some 'w' words need to be spelt with extra care.

14 'Qu', 'qua', and 'que' words

Aim:
to look at the spelling patterns 'qu', 'qua' and 'que'

A | 'QU'

English words never have the letter '**q**' by itself. We always use '**qu**':

★ queen   quiz   quick   quiet   quack   quit

The following words all have 'qu' in the middle. Write them, using the 'Study, Cover, Write, Check' method from Unit 1. Then choose the best words from the list to complete the sentences below.

square   equipment   equal   earthquake   inquiry   liquid   request
require   aquarium   frequently   equator   inquisitive   conquest

1. A _____ has four sides which are all _____ in length.
2. My _____ little sister never stops asking me questions.
3. A fish tank is called an _____ because 'aqua' is Latin for water.
4. Bob and Bill _____ some _____ for their camping trip.
5. I rang the _____ office to find out how _____ the buses run on a Sunday.

B | 'QUA'

In Unit 13 you looked at how '**w**' changes vowels. '**Q**' has the sound /kw/ so it does the same. The short /ŏ/ sound after '**qu**' is usually spelt with the letter '**a**'.

Read the jumbled words and meanings in the box below, listening to the vowel sound /ŏ/. Write the words and their correct meanings next to one another, for example: quality – how good something is.

'QUA' WORDS	MEANINGS
quality	four babies born together
quantity	how good something is
quads	a fruit drink
quarrel	a group of Air Force planes and pilots
quarry	amount
squash	crouch down with knees bent
squadron	an argument or squabble
squat	place where rock or stone is dug out

C | '-QUE'

Did you know that the word 'disco' comes from the French word discothèque (pronounced 'disco-teck')?

Several French words using the letters 'que' to spell the /k/ sound at the end of a word are now part of the English language.

Add the letters '**-que**' to the incomplete words and write these sentences:

1. A Moslem place of worship is called a mos———.
2. My sister bought an old silver spoon from an anti——— shop.
3. Mum wrote a che——— to pay the telephone bill.
4. If something is as pretty as a picture it could be called 'pictures———'.

Fill these gaps with a rhyming '**-que**' word from the sentences above.

a. 'Neck' rhymes with _____.
b. 'Week' rhymes with _____.
c. 'Desk' rhymes with _____.
d. 'Kiosk' rhymes with _____.

D | QWERTY!

Once there was an English teacher who told her Year 7 class that no real word is spelt with just 'q'. It must always be followed by 'u'. She was so sure of her facts that she promised £5 to anyone who could find a real English word which had 'q' but no 'u'. She'd been doing this for about 20 years and had never had to pay up ... until recently! It was 12-year-old Andrew who caught her out. He looked in his brand new dictionary and found the word '**qwerty**'.

Languages change all the time and 'qwerty' is a new word made up to describe the keyboard of a computer. Can you think where the word came from? Is the word 'qwerty' in your dictionary? Do you think it counts as a real word?

Follow-on: If you are unsure about any of the words in this unit, put them in your Personal Spelling Dictionary.

> **Key point –** In all real English words 'q' must be followed by 'u'.

15 There, their, they're & to, too, two

Aim:
to learn some common words which are often misspelt

A | THERE, THEIR, THEY'RE

Make sure you know the difference between **there**, **their**, and **they're**.

There is the most commonly used word. Use it:

★ with words like 'is', 'are' and 'was'
★ to mean a place.

Write these sentences, putting **there** in the gaps.

1. Umad lives over _____ , behind the sports field.
2. I don't know whether _____ is life in outer space but _____'s no doubt I'd like to travel _____ to find out.

Use **their** when it means 'belonging to them'.

Write these sentences, putting **their** in the gaps.

3. They've forgotten _____ games kit again –
   they'd forget _____ heads if they weren't screwed on.
4. The girls got dirt on _____ shirts and _____ skirts.

Look again at the second sentence and underline every '**ir**' pattern. Learn the sentence off by heart. It will help you remember when to use 'their'.

Use **they're** when it's short for 'they are'.

Write these sentences, putting **they're** in the gaps.

5. I don't fancy those chips – _____ too greasy.
6. _____ not coming to the disco because _____ going to Jan's party.

Write out the passage below choosing from **there**, **their** and **they're**.

It's pitch black and I can't see a thing but I'm sure _____ is somebody _____. In fact _____'s more than one. I can hear _____ footsteps even though _____ trying to be quiet. Now _____ much closer. I can hear _____ voices and I can even smell _____ aftershave. I'm creeping back to the door, hoping _____ not going to hear me. Made it! I sure am glad to be out of _____!

B | TO, TOO, TWO

Make sure you know the difference between **to, two,** and **too.**

To is the most commonly used word. Use it:

★ to point the way to a place
★ to point the way to an action.

Use **two** when it means the number 2.

Write these sentences, choosing from **to** or **two**:

1 I'd love _____ travel _____ outer space _____ find out if other life exists.

2 If _____ pet mice were kept together could the result be _____ hundred babies in _____ the space of _____ months?

Use **too** like this:

★ when it means **too** much or **too** many
★ when it means 'as well as'.

Write these sentences, putting **too** in the gaps:

3 Dad complains when I play my CDs _____ loudly and _____ often.

4 I wanted to watch that film _____, but mum said it was _____ violent.

5 Rattlesnakes are poisonous. Scorpions, _____, are poisonous.

Write this passage choosing from **to, too** and **two.**

The Brighton lifeboat had __ be launched last night __ rescue __ young lads who had been trapped on a sandbank for over __ hours.
It was a stormy night and the sea was __ rough for such a small boat.
Their dog was with them __ and all were soaked __ the skin.
The lifeboat crew said the lads were far __ young __ be out alone in such conditions.

Key point – Think before you write *there, their* or *they're* and *to, two* or *too.*

16 'Ou' words

Aim:
to learn words with the letters 'ou'

A | 'OU' AND 'OW'

The letter pattern '**ou**' spells several different sounds. In many words '**ou**' spells the vowel sound you hear in **out**, **house** and **sound**.

Beware!

This sound can also be spelt with the letters '**ow**'. The following rules will help you remember whether to use '**ou**' or '**ow**'. Write the rules and words in your book, filling in the gaps.

1 Use '**ow**' at the end of a word or the end of a syllable:

> ★ cow   now   h__   b__   power   sh__er   fl__er   t__er
> towel   v__el   all__

2 Use '**ow**' before '**n**' and '**l**':

> ★ down   t__n   cr__n   dr__n   fr__n
> owl   h__l   gr__l   sc__l   f__l (meaning 'hens')

3 Use '**ou**' for most other words:

> ★ pound   b__nd   ar__nd   gr__nd
> shout   sp__t   sc__t   spr__t
> bounce   p__nce   tr__nce   ann__nce
> count   m__nt   f__ntain   m__ntain

Write down these rule breaking words: **crowd, crowded, crowding, foul** (meaning 'bad, evil, nasty').

B | 'OU' AS A SHORT SOUND

In a few words, the letters '**ou**' are used to spell the short sound /ŭ/. Match up the beginnings and endings of these muddled sentences and write them correctly.

1 My youngest cousin is   a house in the country.
2 The young couple have bought   to touch his friend's pet snake.
3 Please may I have a double helping   to encourage them to flourish.
4 Patrick plucked up enough courage   in trouble with the police.
5 Water your plants   of that nourishing soup.

C | 'OU' AS A LONG SOUND

In a very few words the /oo/ sound is spelt with the letters '**ou**'. Read the following sentences and find all the words that have '**ou**' saying /oo/, as in 'you'. Write those words.

1 You can use this coupon to get money off packets of vegetable soup.
2 The dance troupe will now perform their latest routine.
3 The youth group helped the wounded rock climber to find a safer route down.

D | 'OU' WITH 'R'

The letter '**r**' can have a strange effect on the '**ou**' pattern – the /or/ sound is spelt '**our**' in a few words.

Give the answers to these clues by filling in the gaps with '**our**'. Write the words.

1 A number. F_____
2 Tip liquid out. P____
3 Play tennis on it. C____t
4 Part of a meal. C____se
5 Belonging to you. Y____
6 Be sad at someone's death. M_____n

Write *one* sentence which contains at least three of the '**our**' words.

Look back over your work and decide which of the '**ou**' words you need to practise. Put these in your Personal Spelling Dictionary.

Follow-on: Work in pairs and test each other on some of the '**ou**' words in this unit.

> **Key point –** The letters '**ou**' appear in all sorts of words, and make several different sounds.

COPYMASTER 16A/B

17 'Ough' words

Aim:
to look at the spelling of' 'ough' words

A | 'OUGH' WORDS

Many useful words are spelt with the '**ough**' pattern.

Practise writing '**ough**' several times. Use cursive writing and, as you write, say the letter names quietly.

Read these sentences, looking for the '**ough**' words:

1. It was his tough luck to get a puncture on the last lap of the race.
2. Bread dough is made by mixing flour, water and yeast.
3. Read right through the exam paper before you start.
4. Most farms have a plough and a trough.
5. Though very cross, he still answered politely.
6. The sea was rough enough to make many passengers sick.
7. Dad, my cough really is too bad for me to go to school!
8. The main branch of a tree is called a bough.

The letters '**ough**' can make many different sounds. Look back at the sentences above. Find and write all the '**ough**' words which rhyme with these words:

1. 'Snow' rhymes with dough and .... (2)
2. 'Scoff' rhymes with .... (2)
3. 'How' rhymes with .... (2)
4. 'Blue' rhymes with .... (1)
5. 'Stuff' rhymes with .... (3)

B | 'THOROUGH' AND 'THOROUGHLY'

These '**ough**' words are thoroughly difficult! Learn them by splitting them into syllables:

★ **tho-rough**   and   **tho-rough-ly**.

Write each word three times, naming the letters as you write.

Write these two sentences with your own endings:

1. I am thoroughly ...
2. My best friend is thoroughly ...

C USING 'OUGH' WORDS

Here are 14 '**ough**' words. Read them and choose the six words you think you are most likely to need in your writing.

| through | cough | trough | plough | bough | rough | tough | enough |
| thorough | borough | thoroughly | dough | though | although |

Now write six sentences, one for each word you have chosen. Add a suffix to any of the words if you wish.

D 'OUGHT' AND 'AUGHT' WORDS

These words have '**ough**' + '**t**' = '**ought**'. They all rhyme with 'sort'.

★ **ought   bought   brought   fought   nought   thought**

Write these sentence pairs, putting an '**ought**' word in each gap. You can use the same word twice. (Choose carefully between 'bought' and 'brought'.)

1. Jim _____ the washing in when the rain started. How _____ ful of him.
2. I _____ not to have _____ with my little brother this morning. I've _____ him a Mars bar to say I'm sorry.
3. Sue _____ _____ times ten was ten. She _____ to know better.
4. Write a sentence of your own using the word **drought** (meaning lack of rain).

The letters '**augh**' can say /or/ or /arf/:

★ **caught   taught   daughter   naughty   draught   laugh**

Spot the '**augh**' words in these sentences and write them.

5. Mum caught her naughty daughter and taught her to behave.
6. To get slaughtered at draughts is no laughing matter.

> **Key point –** Take extra care with the 'ough' and 'augh' words.

Suffixing: When to drop the letter 'e'

Aim:
to find out when to drop the letter 'e' from a root word

A | REVISION

When you add a **vowel** suffix to a root word with a short vowel sound, make sure that there is a 'wall' of two consonants to protect the short vowel from attack.

Copy and complete this table:

ROOT WORD	ADD THIS SUFFIX	RESULT
zap	ing	zapping
shift	ed	
hid	en	
jog	er	
jug	ful	
rub	ed	

B | THE HELPFUL SUFFIXES

tape	ride
stone	cure
shake	

Look at the words in the box. They have only *one* consonant between the vowels. This gives the first vowel a *long* sound.

When you add a vowel suffix to a root word ending in 'e', you can usually drop that 'e'. The first vowel sound will still be long because the vowel in the suffix will do the job of the 'e' for it. Read these examples:

tape + ing = **t a p i n g**

ride + er = **r i d e r**

stone + y = **s t o n y**

Copy and complete this table:

ROOT WORD	SUFFIX	RESULT
joke	er	joker
slide	ing	
smoke	y	
use	ing	
shine	y	
race	ing	
late	ish	
complete	ed	

C | THE UNHELPFUL SUFFIXES

If the suffix begins with a consonant you must *keep* the final 'e' of the root word. This is because there is no new vowel to take its place and do its job. For example:

★ safe + ty = safety   life + less = lifeless   hope + ful = hopeful

Copy and complete this table. Take care! Some are vowel suffixes and some are consonant suffixes.

ROOT WORD	SUFFIX	RESULT
care	ing	
use	ful	
close	ness	
wise	ly	
tube	less	
shade	y	
ripe	ish	
amuse	ment	

D | PROOFREADING

There are several suffixes missing in these sentences. Write the sentences correctly.

1. Vicky is drive her mum's new sports car.
2. When you have translate this into French I will mark it.
3. This new shampoo make my hair so love and shine.
4. He's been in hide for years so trying to find him would be use.
5. I was so scare I was shake.

Follow-on: Write some sentences like those in section D above and give them to a friend to correct. Check the work.

> **Key point –** If you add a vowel suffix to a word which ends in a silent 'e', you normally drop the 'e'. When adding a consonant suffix, keep the 'e'.

19 Silent letters

Aim:
to practise the words which contain silent letters

A GHOSTS FROM THE PAST

In some words, you must remember to include letters which have no sound in that word. Write these words, then draw a circle around the letters which have no sound:

★ ghost   lamb   know   column   write   talk   thistle

Where do these silent letters come from? Why are they there?

A long time ago, some of these letters did have a sound but, because the sounds were difficult to say, they died out. Only their ghosts remain.

B WRITE THE SILENT LETTERS

Write out each of the bold incomplete words in the following lists, putting in the silent letters. Then write them out again, as answers to the clues in the questions. You may not need all the words.

Silent 'w'

-rote   -rap   -rist   -ren
-rong   -reck   -riggle   ans-er

a Opposite of right. _____
b Used a pen. _____
c Smallest British bird. _____
d Twist and turn. _____
e Cover up. _____
f Between hand and arm. _____

Silent 'k'

-nee   -nife   -nobbly   -new
-nowledge   -nock   -not

a Use for cutting. _____
b Bang. _____
c Joint between thigh and calf. _____
d Information, understanding. _____
e Covered in bumps. _____
f Use to join ropes. _____

Silent 'b'

clim-   thum-   com-   bom-
crum-   de-t   dum-

a Small bits of bread or cake. _____
b One on each hand. _____
c Amount of money owing. _____
d Unable to speak. _____
e Brush and _____
f To go up. _____

Silent 't'

Chris-mas   lis-en   fas-en   cas-le
whis-le   this-le

a Thorny plant. _____
b Celebration of Christ's birthday. _____
c Join together. _____
d Use your ears. _____
e Sound made by blowing. _____
f Fortified building. _____

Silent 'l'

Vowel sound /ar/: ca-m   pa-m   ha-f   ca-f
Vowel sound /or/: wa-k   ta-k   sta-k   cha-k

(a) Two quarters. _____
(b) Coconuts grow on it. _____
(c) Use it on a blackboard. _____
(d) Young animal. _____
(e) Part of a plant. _____
(f) Quiet and still. _____

Silent 'h'

g-ost   -our   -onest   ex-austed   ve-icle   g-astly

(a) Extremely tired. _____
(b) 24 in a day. _____
(c) Terrible. _____
(d) Truthful. _____
(e) Means of transport. _____
(f) Appears in horror stories. _____

C PROOFREADING

Spot the mistakes and write the sentences correctly.

1. Lissen carefully then tell me if you no the anser. (3 mistakes)
2. I onestly thought I saw a gost warking around the casle. (4)
3. The repair man nelt under the veicle to check the exaust pipe. (3)
4. I new I was getting my homework rong so I only rote harf a page. (4)

Follow-on: Use a dictionary and find some words beginning with '**gn**'.
The '**g**' is silent.

> **Key point –** You can't hear silent letters, so use your other senses to remember them by *looking* and *writing*.

20 The sound /s/ spelt with the letter 'c'

Aim:
to practise words with the 'ce' spelling pattern

The letter 'c' has two sounds, which are called *hard* and *soft* sounds.

The *hard* sound is /k/ as in **carrots**, **cabbage** and **cucumber**.

The *soft* sound is /s/ as in **celery**, **cider** and **cyanide** (not good to eat!).

The vowels 'e', 'i' and 'y' are needed to make 'c' say its soft sound.

A | '-CE' AT THE END OF WORDS

'Ce' is often used to spell the /s/ sound at the end of words.

 1 Read these 16 words, then write them in alphabetical order:

★ space twice replace dance fence sentence since introduce
sauce advice <u>piece</u> grace reduce <u>peace</u> reproduce disgrace

Look again at the two words that are underlined. Many people confuse these two words. To help remember them, put these mnemonics in your book:

piece: **peace:**

a **pie**ce of **pie** 'Peace Everywhere
And Caring Everywhere'

B | RHYMING '-ICE' AND '-ISS'

These words all rhyme but the rhyming sound is spelt in two different ways.

★ hiss notice miss justice kiss office
practice bliss service hospice

Sort the words into two columns under the headings on the next page.

WORDS WITH ONE SYLLABLE	WORDS WITH TWO SYLLABLE
hiss	notice

What do you notice? Write a sentence which clearly explains this spelling rule.

C | '-ACE' ENDINGS

These words end with a similar sound to those in part B but are spelt 'ace'.

1 Practise the 'ace' spelling pattern, then add it to these word beginnings:

★ neckl___   pal___   furn___   men___   grim___   surf___   terr___

2 Write a sentence containing three of the '-ace' words.

Notice an 'odd one out': **lettuce**. Write it in a sentence.

D | 'CE' AT THE START OR MIDDLE

When '**ce**' is at the start or middle of a word, you can also hear the letter '**e**'.

1 Read these words, then write them. *Remember: 'Study, Cover, Write, Check'.*

★ cent   centre   celebrate   certain   parcel   decent   cancel   concern

2 Make words by matching a word-part from the left-hand group with one from the right:

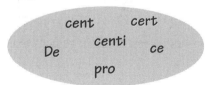

cent   cert   centi   ce   De   pro

cess   ificate   ury   real   metre   cember

E | WORDS BEGINNING WITH 'EX'

These need extra care. Even though '**x**' ends with a /s/ sound, you still need a '**c**' in some words. Put these in your Personal Spelling Dictionary:

★ excellent   exceed   except   excess

Key point – Some words use the letters 'ce' to spell the sound /s/.

21 'Ci' and 'cy'

Aim:
to practise words in which 'i' and 'y' make 'c' say its soft sound /s/.

| A | 'CI' WORDS |

Read these words.

★ city   exciting   pencil   exercises   decimal   civil   cider
medicine   decide   accident   society   vaccination   recipe

Count the number of syllables in each word and write them in three columns under these headings:

TWO SYLLABLES	THREE SYLLABLES	FOUR SYLLABLES
city	exciting	--------------------

Guess what the questions are, by filling in the gaps. Then write the answers to the questions, using two 'ci' words in each answer.

1 Is a –ty likely to have a –nema?
2 Which is better for your health, exer–se or –garettes?
3 Can you use a pen–l to write a re–pe?

The 'science' words

These words have 's' and 'c' together. Choose two of them and write them in sentences.

★ science   scientist   scientific   scissors

The 'circle' words

The word 'circle' comes from the Latin word *circus*, meaning 'ring'. All these words have something to do with a circle or with going round. The meanings have been muddled up. Write each word next to its correct meaning:

circus   the movement of blood around the body
circular   a travelling show which takes place in a round arena
circumference   in the shape of a circle
circulation   a racing track or the path of an electrical current
circuit   the distance around the edge of a circle

B 'CY' WORDS

The letter 'y', when it is acting as a vowel, also makes the letter 'c' say its soft sound.

Read these words. Look in a dictionary for the meanings of any that are new to you.

★ mercy   policy   emergency   agency   currency   cylinder
   cyanide   cygnet   cyclone   fancy   cycling   Cyprus

Write the 'cy' word which is missing from each of the following sentences:

1 A young swan is called a _____.
2 Dollars and cents are the _____ of the USA.
3 After her accident the cyclist was admitted to the _____ department.
4 A _____ is a violent storm with very high winds.
5 Most schools have a _____ for dealing with bullying.
6 _____ is a deadly poison.

C REVISION

The letter 'c' makes the /s/ sound when it is followed by 'e', 'i' or 'y'.

Write out this newspaper report, choosing from 'ce', 'ci' or 'cy' to fill the gaps.

Follow-on: Work with a partner and test each other on words in this unit. If you are unsure of any, add them to your PSD.

The coun—l is con—rned about the high ac—dent rate in the —ty —ntre. It has re—ntly been de—ded that the —ty —ntre streets should be reserved for pedestrians. The poli— is that no vehicles are allowed, ex—pt in an emergen— . Even —clists are banned.

> **Key point –** Some words use 'ci' or 'cy' to spell the sound /s/.

22 The sound /j/ spelt with 'ge'

Aim:
to study words with the sound /j/ spelt with 'g'

The letter '**g**' has two sounds, which are called *hard* and *soft* sounds.

The *hard* sound is /g/ as in **gas**, **gorilla** and **guts**.

The *soft* sound is /j/ as in **gentle**, **giant** and **gymnastics**.

A   -GE AND -DGE ENDINGS

No English word ends with '**j**'. We use '-**ge**' instead, for example:

★ cage   hinge   verge   large   bulge   range

1 Join each beginning to any ending that makes a word.

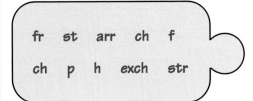 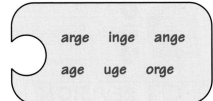

2 Can you think why these words have another letter before '**ge**'?

★ **badge   edge   ridge   splodge   judge**

Find the answers to these clues by choosing the correct word ending from the box.

3 A soft chewy sweet. **f**———

4 A fence made from trees or bushes. **h**———

5 Used for rides down a snowy slope. **sl**———

6 Keep food cold in here. **fr**———

7 Use this to cross the railway line. **br**———

8 A quick sideways movement. **d**———

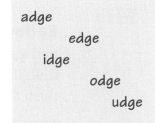

adge
    edge
idge
     odge
      udge

Write all these '**dge**' words, then make up your own clues for three of them.

★ **gadget   knowledge   fidget   midget   widget   lodger   budget**

The /ĭj/ sound at the end of a longer word is usually spelt '-**age**', for example:

★ **cottage   message   manage   cabbage   garage   advantage**

Fill the gaps in the newspaper headlines, using some more words with /ĭj/ spelt '**age**'.

⑨ **Aeroplane Crew Held H_____ by Hijackers**
⑩ S_____ Tiger Escapes from Zoo
⑪ **On Av_____, Teenagers Eat Three Kilos of Chips a Month**
⑫ Yacht Suffers Storm D_____ on Round-the-World V_____
⑬ **C_____ for Sale in Quiet Country V_____**

B 'GE' OR 'JE'?

If the /j/ sound comes at the start or in the middle of the word, it can be '**g**' or '**j**'. The next vowel often helps you decide. Normally we use these patterns:

★ ge gi gy and ja jo ju

① Read these words, then write them, sorting them according to the number of syllables. Highlight or circle the '**ge**' pattern in each word.

★ gentle German genius germ geography gerbil George
generous agent danger emergency angel intelligent
tragedy vegetable

ONE SYLLABLE	TWO SYLLABLES	THREE SYLLABLES	FOUR SYLLABLES
germ	gentle		

② A few words are spelt with the pattern '**je**', for example:

★ jelly jeans subject object jewels jersey jealous

Try and think of some more examples with a friend.

Follow-on: Make up some newspaper headlines using words from this section.

> **Key point –** Always use '-ge' or '-dge' for /j/ at the end of words. Learn by looking to see which other words need 'ge'.

23 More soft 'g' words: 'gi' and 'gy'

Aim:
to study words with the 'gi' and 'gy' patterns

You know that 'e' usually makes 'g' say /j/. The vowels 'i' and 'y' also normally make 'g' say its soft sound /j/.

A | TRUE OR FALSE?

Write down the number of each statement, then write 'true', 'false' or 'maybe' next to it.

1. A giraffe can grow to over five metres tall.
2. Giant pandas are very common animals.
3. A person who moves quickly and easily is agile.
4. The engine of the Saturn moon rocket was equal to 50 jumbo jets.
5. Fragile means very tough.
6. Magic shows make good television programmes.
7. The margin goes at the bottom of the page.
8. Penguins can be found in both Arctic and Antarctic regions.

Now look back at the sentences and write down every word that contains 'gi'.

B | 'GI' WORDS

Match up the beginning of each word with its correct ending. Then complete the sentences below using the words you have made.

> gi   gin   im   regi
> apol   re   tr   magis

> ogise   gantic   ster   agic
> ligion   ger   trate   agine

1. There has been a _____ accident on the mountain.
2. In some schools, form teachers take the _____ on a notebook computer.
3. The root of the _____ plant is used in curries.
4. Can you _____ how I felt?
5. The Titanic was a _____ passenger ship which hit an iceberg.
6. Don't you think you ought to _____?
7. The _____ of many early civilisations involved sun-worship.
8. The _____ fined Julie for riding her bike with no lights.

C | 'GY' WORDS

Only a few words have '**gy**' at the beginning or in the middle. Find and write the '**gy**' words in these sentences:

1 Travelling people were sometimes called gypsies.
2 The pyramids of Egypt were one of the 'Seven Wonders of the World'.
3 A gyroscope is a spinning wheel set in a frame.
4 Write the word **gym** with each of these endings:

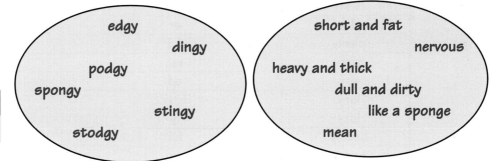

gym + nastics
nast
nasium
khana

Choose one of the words you have made and write it in a sentence.

The letters '**gy**' are more often found at the end of words, making the sound /je/, for example:

★ **energy** **apology** **strategy** (meaning 'plan')

5 The following '**gy**' words are all adjectives. Their meanings have been muddled up. Sort them out and write each adjective next to its meaning. If you are unsure, check in a dictionary.

edgy

dingy

podgy

spongy

stingy

stodgy

short and fat

nervous

heavy and thick

dull and dirty

like a sponge

mean

Follow-on: Work with a partner and test each other on some of the words in this unit.

> **Key point –** The /jĭ/ and /jĭ/ sounds are usually spelt with 'gi' or 'gy', and /jē/ on the end of a word is 'gy'.

24 Suffixing: changing 'y' to 'i'

Aim:
to know when to change 'y' and 'i'

A 'Y' TO 'I'

All these words end with the letter '**y**' used as a vowel. Each word has a consonant just before the vowel.

★ marry   heavy   plenty   copy   fry   dirty   beauty   tricky   spy

When you add a suffix to words like these you must first change the '**y**' to '**i**'.

Example: **happy + est = happ~~y~~iest**

This rule applies to all suffixes except '**ing**' and '**ish**', even consonant suffixes.

Copy and complete this table:

ROOT WORD	CHANGE 'Y' TO 'I' AND ADD THIS SUFFIX	RESULT
marry	ed	married
heavy	ness	heaviness
funny	est	
dry	er	
plenty	ful	
tricky	est	
spy	ed	
lazy	ness	
lazy	ly	
beauty	ful	
happy	er	
lovely	est	
dusty	er	

When you add the suffix '**s**' you must change the '**y**' to '**ies**'; for example:

★ fly ➡ flies   lorry ➡ lorries   dictionary ➡ dictionaries

Write these words correctly after adding the suffix '**s**'.

★ story   carry   cry   puppy   duty   family   galaxy   factory   enemy

B   EXCEPTIONS

There are two cases where you do not need to change the letter 'y':

1 English words do not have two 'i's together so we don't change the 'y' when the suffix begins with 'i'. Write these examples:

> ★   hurry ➡ hurrying   baby ➡ babyish

2 Some words have a vowel before the 'y'. It would look silly to have too many small vowels together, so we don't change the 'y'. Write these examples:

> ★   stay ➡ stayed   monkey ➡ monkeys   employ ➡ employer

Remember the rules:

★   if the root word has a consonant just before the 'y', change the 'y' to 'i'.
★   don't change when you add '**ing**'.
★   when the suffix is '**s**', change 'y' to '**ies**'.

Work out the results in this table.

ROOT WORD	SUFFIX	RESULT	ROOT WORD	SUFFIX	RESULT
pray	ing		easy	ly	
curry	s		journey	s	
joy	ful		dismay	ed	
supply	ed		pretty	est	
glory	ous		carry	ed	
shady	er		enjoy	ment	
ready	ness		try	s	

Follow-on: Make up some sentences containing words from your 'Result' columns.

> **Key point –** If a word ends in a consonant + y, change the 'y' to 'i' before you add any suffix, except '-ing' or '-ish'.

(side note)
hurriing ✗
fliing ✗
staied ✗
monkeies ✗

Choosing between 'ie' or 'ei'

Aim:
to find out whether to use 'ie' or 'ei'

Ask any adult to tell you a spelling rule and
they will almost certainly say this one:

But is this rule really true? Let's see.

'i' before 'e' except after 'c'.

A | DOES THE RULE WORK?

Here is an example of the suffix rule you
learnt in Unit 24.

★ **Vacancy + 's' = vacancies**

Find the pattern '**ie**' in the word above and look at the letter before it. Does
the rule '**i**' before '**e**' except after '**c**' work here? NO!
The rule here is:

★ **In a suffix, we always use 'ie', even after 'c'.**

Write down these suffix 'sums' and complete them.

**fly + s = _____   fancy + ed = _____   discovery + s = _____
funny + er = _____   emergency + s = _____**

B | THE LONG /ē/ SOUND

Read these words, look carefully at the spelling of the /ē/ sound and sort
them into two sets: '**ie**' words in the first set, '**ei**' words in the second.

chief believe receive field
deceive shield ceiling
conceited fierce brief achieve
receipt relief piece

'IE' WORDS	'EI' WORDS

Choose two words from each set and write your own sentences for them.
Does the original rule work here? Yes, it is:

★ **'i' before 'e' except after 'c' : if the sound is a long /ē/.**

Even here there are a few rule-breakers! Look at the next section.

C | WEIRD WORDS

The rule-breakers are words like:

★ w<u>ei</u>rd   s<u>ei</u>ze   prot<u>ei</u>n

and the names:

★ K<u>ei</u>th   N<u>ei</u>l   Sh<u>ei</u>la.

Use some of the 'weird' words to complete these sentences:

1 _____ believes her children should eat plenty of _____.
2 My friend _____ has a _____ sense of humour.
3 I saw the bank robber _____ the money.

D | 'EI' WORDS

Words with the '**ei**' pattern normally have the long /ā/ sound. Write down the clues and for each one find the '**ei**' word from the box that best fits each clue.

1 Eighteen minus ten.
2 Rudolf.
3 Noise made by a horse.
4 Next door.
5 Heaviness.
6 Covers the face.
7 Snow transport.
8 Rule as king or queen.
9 Full of blood.
10 To control a horse.

reindeer	neigh	weight
reign	rein	eight	veil
sleigh	neighbours	vein

Follow-on: Make up three or four sentences. Each one should contain both an '**ie**' and an '**ei**' word.

> **Key point –** 'i' before 'e' except after 'c' – but only when it rhymes with 'be'. The new version of the rule makes a useful rule, *as long as you remember the exceptions.*

26 More homophones

Aim:
to study the spelling of some more difficult homophones

A | REVISION: WHAT ARE HOMOPHONES?

Homophones are words which sound the same but have different meanings and are spelt differently. Can you remember how they got their name?

To help you remember what you learnt, write out the sentences and fill in the gaps below. The two missing words on each line have *long* vowel sounds, and are homophones.

1. Can you w_____ with your left hand? Turn r_____ at the lights.
2. Please w_____ quietly. Guess the w_____ of the cake.
3. That band plays g_____ music. G_____ the cheese for the sauce.
4. Have you s_____ my best shirt? The film's hero won in the final s_____.

B | A MIXED BAG OF SOUNDS

Each sentence should contain two homophones. Find the missing one from this list and use it to fill the gaps. The first one is done for you.

★ **threw   blew   where   won   seize   heard**
   paws   whether   fare   caught

1. Vicky's **blue** scarf __blew__ away in the strong wind.
2. A herd of elephants could be _____ trumpeting by the lake.
3. Sara ran through the crowd and _____ the ball back to the team.
4. You'll need £1.20 for your bus _____ to the fair-ground.
5. I wouldn't wear those jeans _____ you are going.
6. My kitten will often pause in its step, sit down and lick its _____.
7. It was such a close finish that no-one was sure who had _____ the race.
8. Lifeboat crews show great bravery when they _____ people from stormy seas.
9. Mum wonders _____ she should take the baby out in such cold weather.
10. Those who get _____ shop-lifting could end up in court.

C HOW TO CHOOSE THE RIGHT WORD

Some words give you clues about which choice to make. Look at these two examples:

Knew sounds the same as **new**, so think of another word to help you:

★ 'I **knew** all that gossip – I thought you would **know** too.'

Groan sounds the same as **grown**, so think of another word to help you:

★ 'My, how you've **grown**,' said Nan. 'I've never known anyone **grow** so fast.'

Use this method to help you choose the correct word. Write the sentences:

1. The ambulance **passed/past** us with its siren going.
2. Are we **aloud/allowed** to stay in this lunchtime?
3. At the State Opening of Parliament the Queen sits on a **thrown/throne**.
4. A golden eagle **sword/soared** above the mountain peak.
5. When our car was damaged in an accident we had to **hire/higher** one.

D SPOT THESE ERRORS

Spot the errors in these signs and write the correct version in your book:

To the beech

Do not waist water

Beware of bares

Follow-on: Make up your own mnemonics for words in your PSD.

> **Key point –** Be wary of homophones, and double check them if you are unsure.

27 Stress in words

Aim:
to think about the spelling of neutral vowels

A | HEAR THE STRESS

The a-li-ens in-tend to ex-ter-min-ate ev-er-y a-ttack-er

Captain, our robot says the aliens intend to exterminate every attacker!

Some films have robots in them which speak in computerised voices, giving every syllable the same emphasis. This sounds boring.

In words containing two or more syllables, one of the syllables has a stronger sound than the rest. The strongest syllable is called the *stressed* syllable.

Practise reading the speech bubble in a 'robot' voice. Then read it again in your *normal* voice. Pick out the stressed syllable in each word.

The stressed syllable has been underlined in the words below. Can you hear that it is stronger than the rest?

★ <u>a</u>lien in<u>tend</u> ex<u>ter</u>minate <u>e</u>very at<u>tac</u>ker

You try the following ones. Write the words and say each one in a normal voice. Then underline the stressed syllable in each.

★ pilot expect dictionary underline computer complete

Listen to the *vowels* in the syllables you have marked. Stressed syllables are easy to spell because you can hear the vowel sounds clearly.

B | WEAK SOUNDS

Sometimes the vowel sounds are not so clear. In these words the *unstressed* syllable has been underlined. Say each word in your normal voice and listen to the vowel sounds in the unstressed syllable.

★ hel<u>met</u> <u>at</u>tend dra<u>gon</u> cap<u>tain</u> sel<u>dom</u> <u>des</u>pair lev<u>el</u> <u>col</u>lect

The unstressed vowel has a very weak sound, a bit like a short /ŭ/ sound, or a very soft /er/. The proper name for this very weak vowel sound is the '**schwa**' (pronounced 'shwar' to rhyme with 'car'.)

Some dictionaries use a special symbol to show how to pronounce a word with a 'schwa' sound: /ə/. It looks like the letter 'e' but upside down and back to front.

Say these words and listen for the 'schwa' sound. Then write the words and put the 'schwa' symbol above the vowel that has the 'schwa' sound.

★ **complete   applause   final   sausage
lesson   demand   label   continue**

C HOW TO SPELL THE 'SCHWA' SOUND

Your sense of hearing cannot help you to spell a 'schwa' sound. So how will you cope? Here are some ideas.

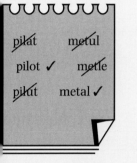

1 Your sense of sight is one of your greatest spelling helpers. If you can hear a 'schwa' sound but can't remember the spelling, try the 'jotter' method:

★ Jot down the spellings you think are possible.
★ Can you see which one **looks** right?
★ Check that your choice is correct and cross out the wrong ones.

2 Try using a 'spelling language'. How did you learn to spell **Wednesday**? Did it help to say 'Wed - **nes** - day'?

Work in pairs and read these words to each other. Then change the way you would normally say them and give any 'schwa' sound a *strong* vowel sound instead.

★ **lemon   certain   balance   difference
independent   pleasant   major**

Now test each other on the spelling of those words.

Follow-on: Look at a page of any book and find words with the 'schwa' sound. Write the words and draw the 'schwa' sign above the weak vowels.

> **Key point –** Take extra care when spelling the 'schwa' sound.

28 Ending with '-er', '-ar' and '-or'

Aim:
to look at the spelling of words ending with the 'schwa' sound

A | HOW 'R' AFFECTS VOWEL SOUNDS

1 The letter 'r' changes the sound of a vowel. Put the vowel + 'r' in the gaps below and write the words.

- **a** **ar**: st—t c—toon al—m m—ket sh—k
- **b** **er**: h—b st—n p—son g—m h—d (*of animals*)
- **c** **ir**: f—st th—d d—t c—cle squ—t
- **d** **or**: st—my rec—d c—ner perf—m rep—t
- **e** **ur**: ch—ch occ— n—se b—st c—ve

2 Now add 'e' to the same patterns. Read aloud the words you make and listen to the endings. Does the vowel sound change?

- **a** **are**: sh— comp— prep— squ— aw—
- **b** **ere**: h— th— wh— w— sinc— interf—
- **c** **ire**: f— vamp— enqu— requ— des—
- **d** **ore**: sn— sw— bef— expl— ign—
- **e** **ure**: c— p— mat— sec— end—
- **f** **ture**: (*a different sound*) cap— mix— fu— tor— adven—

B | 'SCHWA' ENDINGS

Say these words and listen to the last syllable.

★ **singer dancer, actor doctor, sugar collar**

The final syllables all make the same 'schwa' sound. You cannot hear any clear vowel sound and this means you need to take extra care with the spelling.

Most 'schwa' endings are spelt with 'er'. Write the answers to these clues:

1. Someone who writes. **writer.**
2. Someone who swims.
3. Something that toasts.
4. Something that buzzes.
5. More large.
6. More sweet.
7. More loud.
8. More brave.

C   '-OR' ENDINGS

Practise each letter pattern below three times. Then write each set of words.

★ Use '-or' after 'ct' ➡ ctor   : actor doctor collector instructor inspector
★ Use '-or' after 'it' ➡ itor   : visitor editor
★ Use '-or' after 'at' ➡ ator   : calculator operator radiator
★ Use '-or' after 'ess' ➡ essor : professor processor
★ Use '-or' after 'rr' ➡ rror   : error terror horror mirror

Choose from the '-**or**' words above to complete these sentences:

1 The _____ in the _____ film had terrifying make-up.
2 My maths was wrong because I made an _____ on my _____.
3 The safety _____ said the _____ was far too hot.
4 The _____ used a _____ on a long handle to look at my sore throat.

D   '-AR' ENDINGS

We often use '-**ar**' after '**l**'.

1 Practise the '**lar**' pattern three times then write the words:

★ collar dollar cellar circular caterpillar regular popular similar

2 These words also end in '-**ar**'. Write them:

★ calendar vinegar jaguar vulgar beggar sugar peculiar

3 Now choose any three '-**ar**' words and write your own sentence for each.

Follow-on: Put any words you are unsure of in your Personal Spelling Dictionary and make up some mnemonics to help you remember the endings.

An idea to start you off: draw a large outline of a c**ar** and write some of the '-**ar**' words inside it.

> **Key point –** Most 'schwa' endings are spelt with '-er'.
> **Practise and learn the ones that end in '-ar' and '-or'.**

29 Ending with '-ate' and '-ite'

Aim:
to study words which end in '-ate' and '-ite'

A WORDS ENDING IN '-ATE'

Read these words. What letter pattern appears in every word?

★ **date   gate   hate   late   mate   plate   skate   state
suffocate   concentrate   illustrate   translate**

What sound does the letter pattern '**ate**' make? Is the vowel sound long or short?

Write the words using the 'Study, Cover, Write, Check' method. You can hear the long /ā/ sound clearly, which makes them quite easy to spell.

B THE 'SCHWA' SOUND FOR '-ATE'

In Unit 27 you learnt that some words have a very weak vowel sound, the 'schwa', in one syllable.

1 Write these words and mark the weak vowel in each with the special symbol: ə.

★ **helmet   carrot   pilot**

When the 'schwa' sound is followed by /t/ it is often spelt '**ate**'.

2 Read these sentences. Find five words ending in '**ate**' and write them down.

★ The long-distance swimmer was awarded a certificate.
★ It was fortunate for the marathon runner that there was a moderate breeze.
★ Accurate time-keeping is essential in top-level competition.
★ The ultimate aim of many athletes is to win a gold medal.

Say the five '**ate**' words aloud and listen to the 'schwa' sound in the final syllable of each.

3 Read and then practise writing these words, using the 'Study, Cover, Write, Check' method.

★ **deliberate   delicate   immediate   passionate   chocolate**

4 Make up a sentence for each of these words:

★ **approximate   desperate   unfortunate   separate   climate**

C   '-ITE' ENDINGS

The letters '**ate**' are the most common way of spelling the sound /ət/ at the end of a word. However, a few words use the letters '**ite**' to spell this sound.

Find three '**ite**' words from these muddled syllables:

 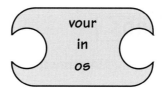 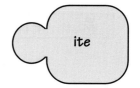

Write these sentences. Use one of the words you have made to fill the gap in each sentence.

1 I'll meet you at half past six _____ the station.
2 Jill's _____ sport is tennis.
3 I'm not wearing those old boots and that's _____!
4 The ball crossed the line so it was _____ a goal.
    (Add a suffix to one of the 'ite' words to fill this gap.)

Follow-on: Look again at all the words in this unit. In your Personal Spelling Dictionary make a note of all the words you feel you need to practise. Warning – you will *definitely* be tested on the word '**definite**'!

> **Key point –** In words of more than one syllable, the sound /ət/ is usually spelt '**ate**'. Remember this rule – but don't forget the '**-ite**' words.

30 'Ph' words

The sound /f/ is usually spelt with just the letter 'f', but:

★ After a short vowel you need 'ff': **staff   cliff   fluff   scoff**
★ Don't forget the 'ugh' words: **enough   rough   tough   cough   laugh**
★ Words which come from the Ancient Greek language use the letters 'ph' instead.

A | 'PH' WORDS

Read the following ten sentences. Which ones *could* be true? Write out those sentences.

1. Elephants can live between 60 and 70 years.
2. Philip's favourite nephew is called Sarah.
3. The US Navy have trained dolphins to detect mines.
4. The team which won the trophy will return home in triumph.
5. 'Paragraph' is another word for sentence.
6. Geography is more interesting than history.
7. The letters PE stand for 'Physical Education'.
8. You could make a graph to show which letter of the alphabet is most used.
9. 'Phantom' is another word for fairy.
10. Pop stars might send autographed photographs to their fans.

Now look back at the sentences and write down all the '**ph**' words you can find.

B | 'F' 'FF' 'GH' 'PH' – WHICH?

Read these sentences saying the sound /f/ in all the gaps. Then write the sentences choosing the correct way to spell the /f/ sound.

You have four choices: **f   ff   gh   ph**

1. Man has __ound that ele__ants are use__ul __or transporting logs over rou__ ground.
2. We all had a good lau__ at a __unny __otogra__ of my ne__ew Christo__er.
3. The geogra__y teacher said that my gra__ showing the rain__all was __ine but one paragra__ of writing was not nearly enou__.

C TEACH YOURSELF SOME GREEK

Inventors and scientists often get ideas from ancient languages when they are choosing new words for their discoveries.

Many of the words below come from Greek. Their meanings have been muddled up. Write each word next to its correct meaning.

1 photograph   Several sentences grouped together.
2 graph   A picture made by letting light into a camera.
3 paragraph   A personally signed name.
4 photocopier   A musical instrument.
5 stereophonic   Sound coming from two speakers.
6 autograph   This sends sound over long distances.
7 telephone   Information in the form of a diagram with blocks or lines.
8 biography   Machine using strong light to copy from an original.
9 microphone   The story of a person's life.
10 saxophone   Attaches to a loudspeaker or recording system.

Look again at the words and their meanings. There are enough clues there to help you translate these Ancient Greek words. Write each Greek word next to its meaning:

phonos   graph   photo

light   sound   writing

Follow-on: Make up some sentences as in section A, and give them to a friend to answer. Use some of these words:

★ elephant   telephone   microphone   dolphin   photograph

Key point – Read the 'ph' words often. This will help to fix them in your memory.

31 When 'ch' sounds like /k/ and /sh/

Aim:
to learn when to use 'ch' to spell the sounds /k/ and /sh/

A | 'TCH' WORDS

You already know how to spell many '**ch**' words. Read these aloud and listen to the sound made by the letters '**ch**':

★ church   coach   approach   chimpanzee
  champion   challenge   cheque

Watch out for the words which need '**tch**'. You normally need '**tch**' if the /ch/ sound comes straight after a short vowel:

★ snatch   catch   fetch   stretch   ditch
  kitchen   blotch   Dutch   butcher

Think of some more '**tch**' words to fill the gaps in these sentences:

1 Please sw_____ off the television.
2 We lost the m_____ by three goals.
3 Pet rabbits are kept in a h_____.
4 Draw a quick sk_____.

Some rule-breakers:

Use only '**ch**' in these short-vowel words. Write them down.

★ rich   such   much   which   attach   detach   sandwich

B | 'CH' FOR /K/ SOUND

In these words '**ch**' has the sound /k/. Most of them come from Ancient Greek.

★ echo   anchor   character   orchestra   ache   chaos   stomach
  school   chemistry   mechanic   technology   choir (pronounced
  'quire')   Christ   Christmas   Christopher   Christine

Write out the passages on the next page, filling in the blanks with some of the 'ch'=/k/ words from the list above.

1. Last year our s_____ drama group put on a musical version of the Charles Dickens story 'A _____ Carol'. A boy called _____ played the main _____ , Scrooge. My sister _____ sang in the _____ and I played the drums in the _____ .

2. Although it was pitch black, the ship's crew knew they were dangerously close to the cliffs as they could hear the e_____ of their voices. All was ch_____ on board as they battled to drop the _____ in the stormy seas.

3. Samantha does not enjoy science subjects and particularly hates ch_____. However, she is very good at Design and _____. When she leaves _____ she would like to train as a car _____.

4. Christopher ate six chocolate cakes at the_____ party and woke up in the night with a bad _____ _____

C | 'CH' FOR /SH/ SOUND

In these words of French origin the /sh/ sound is spelt with '**ch**'.

★ **chef   machine   parachute   brochure
chauffeur   champagne   moustache**

Read the clues below and write the word that fits each one.

1. Ask him to cook you a special meal.
2. Don't jump out of an aeroplane without one of these.
3. Drink this at a special celebration.
4. He might drive a rock star to a party.
5. Look in here to choose your holiday.
6. Shave around this.
7. Switch this on to do your washing.

Follow-on: Use a dictionary to find some more words with '**ch**' saying /k/ or /sh/. Write each one in a sentence to show its meaning.

> **Key point –** Remember that some words use '**ch**' to spell the /k/ and /sh/ sounds.

32 '-tion' and '-cian' endings

Aim:
to practise words ending in '-tion' and to learn other ways of spelling the same sound

A INTRODUCING '-TION'

Read these words and listen to the sound in the final syllable of each:

★ action   nation   infection   instruction

Words with the '-**tion**' ending are often quite long. This means you must be careful to write every syllable in the word.

Draw three columns like this:

TWO SYLLABLE WORDS	THREE SYLLABLE WORDS	FOUR SYLLABLE WORDS

Now read these words and write them under the correct headings. Beware! There are two words in this list which will not go in any of your columns.

★ introduction   station   option   direction   pollution   education
confirmation   obstruction   imagination   attention   fiction
generation   completion   mention   competition   organisation

Write some more '-**tion**' words by filling in the missing vowels:

1. The number of people in a town is its p-p-l-t—n.
2. Gita gave the police a detailed d-scr-pt—n of the bank robber.
3. This leaflet gives you all the -nf-rm-t—n on the theme park.
4. Mark has a huge c-ll-ct—n of Star Trek pictures and models.
5. When the bricklayers walked out, all c-nstr-ct—n work stopped.
6. Jemma has gained pr-m-t—n to the job of manager.

B FROM VERBS TO NOUNS

You can make nouns from verbs by adding the suffix '-**tion**'. Sometimes the root word has to change. Match up the verbs and nouns in the boxes on the next page and write them like this: **donate ➔ donation**

VERBS		
donate	compete	prepare
intend	elect	add
hesitate		complete
	solve	

NOUNS		
election	intention	donation
competition	hesitation	completion
preparation		solution
	addition	

C '-CIAN' ENDINGS

When a word describes a person's occupation, it is sometimes spelt '-**cian**'.

Read these words, then write them. (Remember: 'Study, Cover, Write, Check')

★ electrician   musician   optician   magician   politician   beautician
mathematician   technician   physician

Can you work out why the words above have this strange spelling? Think of their root words. Two clues:

★ **A musician deals with _____.   A magician deals with _____.**

Write these sentences using whichever '-**cian**' word you think is the best fit.

1 Sanjay plays the guitar and wants to be a professional _____.
2 Kelly enjoys debates and her ambition is to be a _____.
3 Alex would love to be a _____ working on a cruise ship.
4 Vicky enjoys tricks and would like a stage career as a _____.
5 Science is Tom's best subject and he wants to be an _____.

Remember: If you are unsure about any of the words in this unit, put them in your spelling dictionary. Include these two rule-breakers:

★ fashion   cushion

What is odd about those two words?

Follow-on: Make up an exercise to test a friend on '-**tion**' and '-**cian**' spelling choices.

> **Key point –** In most cases the /shən/ ending is spelt with '-**tion**', but remember to use '-**cian**' for occupations.

33 '-sion' endings

Aim:
to look at words which end in '-sion'

A | '-SION' AND '-TION'

Another quite common ending is '**-sion**'. With some words you can tell whether to use the '**-sion**' spelling or '**-tion**' because the sound is slightly different.

Say the following words aloud and listen *very* carefully to the final syllable. In set A the sound is /shən/, but in set B it is more of a buzzing sound, like /zhən/.

SET A: condition   friction   mention   decoration   definition   invention

SET B: explosion   collision   vision   confusion revision   supervision
       persuasion   television   decision   evasion   provision   seclusion

Write these sentences, completing them with a '**-sion**' word:

1. The players argued but the referee's _____ was final.
2. The word _____ comes from 'tele' meaning 'from afar' and
   '_____' meaning 'sight'.
3. It is sensible to allow plenty of time for _____ before exams.
4. The _____ between the car and the petrol tanker caused a huge
   _____.

B | TEST YOUR LISTENING SKILLS

You decide on the ending of the incomplete word in each of the following sentences. Read the sentence and say the completed word aloud, listening carefully to the last syllable.

If the sound is /shən/, spell it with the '**-tion**' ending.
If the sound is /zhən/, spell it with the '**-sion**' ending.

1. In maths, a sum in which you add is an **addi**_____ sum.
2. In maths, a sum in which you divide is a **divi**_____ sum.
3. The attacking army launched an **inva**_____.
4. The injured footballer may need an **opera**_____.
5. The great **occa**____ was celebrated with a huge firework display.
6. **Ero**____ by the waves is causing the collapse of those cliffs.

C | '-SSION' WORDS

So far you have learnt these two facts about the /shən/ and /zhən/ sounds:

★ The /shən/ sound is usually spelt '**-tion**', as in **instruction** and sometimes '**-cian**' as in **musician**.

★ The /zhən/ sound is spelt '**-sion**', as in **explosion**.

Now for the confusion!

★ The /shən/ sound is also sometimes spelt with '**-sion**', often with '**ss**'.

Read these words and look in a dictionary for the meaning of any that are new to you:

★ mission   discussion   depression   confession   passion
session   expression   permission   transmission   profession
admission   compassion   percussion   impression

D | WHICH '-SSION' WORDS?

Which '**-ssion**' words fit best in the spaces? There are some clues to help you.

Have you girls got p_____ to be in the music room at lunchtime? And who said you could play with the p_____ instruments? From the guilty e_____ on your faces I get the i_____ that you know very well that you should not be here. And don't mutter under your breath when I am talking to you. We are not going to have a d_____ about who is right. It would be far better if you just made an a_____ of guilt. In all my years in the teaching p_____ I have never met a more unruly bunch of girls!

Key point – Use your eyes to remember some of these difficult words. If you read them several times and look at them carefully, your memory will 'photograph' the correct spelling.

---

34 Prefixes

A **prefix** is a group of letters put at the beginning of a root word to change its meaning, for example:

★ over + time = overtime   dis + appear = disappear   un + even = uneven

A | WORD PREFIXES

Some prefixes are words in themselves and their meaning is clear. Match each prefix below to *two* root words and write the result:

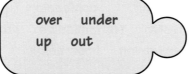

over   under   up   out

stairs   ground   grown   right   burst   wear   side   charge

B | PREFIXES FOR OPPOSITE MEANING

Some prefixes mean 'not' and make the root words mean the opposite, for example:

★ un + steady   dis + agree   in + complete

Find the incomplete words in this passage. Write them in full, choosing from the prefixes '**un**-', '**dis**-' and '**in**-' to complete the words.

Your bedroom is a __grace. You tidy it so __frequently that it's __credible that you can ever find anything. The carpet has completely __appeared under an __limited number of clothes and those mouldy socks are giving off a most __pleasant smell. I know you want to be __dependent but __fortunately, if you carry on __obeying me, I shall be forced to come in here and __infect the place from top to bottom.

C | WHAT DOES THE PREFIX MEAN?

The prefix '**tele**-' comes from an Ancient Greek word meaning 'far off'.

Add the prefix '**tele**-' to these root words:

★ phone   scope   vision

Write each set of words on the next page, then guess the meaning of the prefix.

1. reappear   reread   reproduce   rebuild
   re means _____
2. submarine   subway   submerge
   sub means _____
3. preview   prefix   precooked   prepack
   pre means _____
4. supervisor   supersonic   superhuman
   super means _____
5. anticlockwise   anticlimax   antifreeze   antisocial
   anti means _____

6. misprint   misspell   misbehave   misjudge
   mis means _____

D PREFIXES THAT MUST CHANGE

Some prefixes have to change when added to a word, to make the new word easier to say.

The prefix '**in-**' means 'not'. Suppose you want to say something is not **legal**: it is hard to get your tongue around 'in-legal', so the prefix '**in-**' changes to '**il-**' and you say '**illegal**':

★ 'in-mediate' becomes '**immediate**'
★ 'in-resistible' becomes '**irresistible**'

Take care! These words need a double letter, because one belongs to the prefix and one belongs to the root word.

Use '**im-**' before words that start with '**p**': for example, **improper**.

Complete these words with the correct letter:

1. i-moral
2. i-regular
3. i-logical
4. i-moveable
5. i-passable
6. i-legible
7. i-possible
8. i-polite
9. i-responsible

> **Key point –** Recognising prefixes will help you to spell many long words.

COPYMASTER 34

77

35 '-able' and '-ible' endings

Aim:
to find out when to use the suffix '-able' and when to use '-ible'

The suffixes '-**able**' and '-**ible**' mean 'can be done'. For example:

★ **kickable** means 'can be kicked', as in 'This penalty is kickable'.
★ **forcible** means 'can be forced', as in 'We are locked out but the window is forcible'.

There is no easy rule to help you remember whether to use '-**able**' or '-**ible**'. But most words have the '-**able**' ending. So if you simply learn the few '**ible**' words you are likely to need, you can remember that almost all the others use the '-**able**' ending.

A THE SUFFIX '-ABLE'

These sentences are only partly complete. Write out the start of each sentence, underline the '-**able**' word and then make up your own ending.

1 Will you be available for work on ....?
2 The road is no longer passable because ....
3 How comfortable is ....?
4 My most memorable birthday was ....
5 It was not very sociable of you to ....
6 Martin's hair was noticeable because ....

Sometimes you can spot a verb as part of the '-**able**' word. When you add the suffix '-**able**' to a verb, you change the verb into an adjective. Copy this table, choosing the best word from the box to follow each '-**able**' adjective:

ROOT VERBS	'-ABLE' ADJECTIVES
like	a likeable _____
cure	a curable _____
read	a readable _____
excuse	an excusable _____
climb	a climbable _____

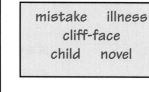

mistake   illness
cliff-face
child   novel

Make your own table like the one opposite. Add the suffix '**-able**' to these words:

★ **prefer   depend   consider   print   use** *(drop the 'e')*

Write these sentences choosing one of your '**-able**' words to complete each one:

1 This CD player is broken beyond repair; it is no longer _____.
2 The words used by the rock star were not _____ in a family newspaper.
3 A _____ person is one who keeps a promise.
4 A _____ amount of snow fell overnight.
5 A pizza with plenty of toppings is _____ to one with only cheese.

B | THE SUFFIX '-IBLE'

These are the '**-ible**' words you are most likely to need. Practise writing them.

★ **audible   horrible   possible   flexible   edible   visible   terrible responsible   permissible   legible   sensible   incredible**

Look again at your list and write the '**-ible**' answers to these clues:

1 Can be done.
2 Can be bent without breaking.
3 Fit to eat.
4 Allowed.
5 Neatly written.
6 Can be seen.
7 Unbelievable.
8 Can be heard.
9 Two words meaning 'dreadful'.
10 Two words meaning 'reliable'.

Follow-on: Write three or four sentences, each one containing both an '**-able**' and an '**-ible**' word.

Key point – Learn the '-ible' words. Use '-able' for nearly all the others. If you are unsure, use a dictionary or a spell-checker, then practise the correct spelling.

36 '-ous' endings

Aim:
to practise adjectives with the '-ous' ending

A '-OUS'

When you hear the /us/ sound at the end of an adjective, spell it '-**ous**'.

1 Practise the '-**ous**' pattern several times.

2 Match up each adjective from the left-hand box with one of the nouns from the right-hand box and write them together.

Example: a tremendous performance

poisonous	marvellous
enormous	famous
jealous	nervous

kitten	present
mountain	friend
snake	singer

3 Complete these words with '-**ous**' and add a suitable noun of your own to the blank space next to the word.

a gener___ _____   a danger___ _____

a monstr___ _____   a fabul___ _____

B '-OUS' WITH VOWELS BEFORE IT

Sometimes the vowels '**e**', '**i**' or '**u**' come just before '-**ous**'. This often gives the word an extra syllable.

Practise writing these letter patterns three times, then make up sentences for each of the words listed below.

LETTER PATTERN	WORDS
eous	hideous miscellaneous
uous	strenuous continuous
ious	various mysterious

These words have the '-**eous**' pattern but they are a little different.

★ gorgeous   courageous

The letter '**e**' does not make an extra syllable but it *does* have a reason for being there. Can you think why the '**e**' needs to be there?

Write this sentence putting the '-**geous**' words in the gaps:

★ 'Isn't he _____ ?' whispered Emma to her friend, as the _____ hero of the film saved an entire city from destruction by aliens.

C | 'CI' BEFORE '-OUS'

In these words the sound /sh/ before the '-**ous**' ending is spelt with the letters '**ci**':

Write these phrases, choosing the more suitable of the two adjectives suggested:

1 a **spacious/precious** old necklace **3** a **vicious/gracious** guard dog
2 a **suspicious/precious** noise **4** a **ferocious/delicious** pizza

Practise the word '**anxious**' by writing it in these sentences:

5 Mum was so _____ when my brother was late coming home.
6 There was no need for her to be _____ as he had simply missed the bus.

D | A HIDEOUS TALE

Write the first paragraph of a horror story. Make the atmosphere really spooky by using at least eight of the '-**ous**' words listed below. Add suffixes if you wish: **anxious + ly = anxiously, courageous + ly = courageously**

★ hideous mysterious famous enormous vicious ferocious
nervous cautious suspicious anxious jealous curious
poisonous courageous dangerous monstrous

Follow-on: Work with a friend and test each other on words from this unit. Add the hardest ones to your PSD.

Key point – The /us/ sound at the end of adjectives is spelt '**ous**'.

---

37 Adding suffixes to longer words

Aim:
to learn how to add vowel suffixes to words of more than one syllable

In Unit 11 you learnt the rule about needing two consonants to protect a short vowel when adding a vowel suffix.

However, if the root word has more than *one* syllable, the rules are slightly different.

A LISTEN FOR STRESS

Look back at Unit 27. You learnt that *longer* words have one syllable with a stronger sound than the others. The strong syllable is called the *stressed* syllable.

In these words the stressed syllable has been underlined. Read the words:

★ <u>su</u>gar spa<u>ghe</u>tti <u>sau</u>sages po<u>ta</u>toes maca<u>ro</u>ni <u>mar</u>malade

1 Write these words and underline the stressed syllable in each:

★ giraffe kangaroo buffalo monkey rhinoceros hippopotamus

Sometimes the unstressed syllable has a weak vowel sound. Read these words and listen for the weak vowel:

★ trumpet guitar saxophone recorder triangle

2 Write these words, find the weak vowel sound and put the 'schwa' mark (ə) above it:

★ parrot flamingo vulture falcon eagle

B DOUBLE OR NOT?

These words all end with one vowel + one consonant. The *second* syllable is stressed and you can hear a clear *short* vowel sound:

★ for<u>get</u> sub<u>mit</u> be<u>gin</u> up<u>set</u> com<u>mit</u> ex<u>pel</u>

If you can hear a short vowel sound, it needs to be protected when we add a vowel suffix, so we must double the last letter, for example:

★ forget + ing = forge<u>tt</u>ing submit + ing = submi<u>tt</u>ing

Now add the suffix '**-ing**' to: begin upset commit expel

These words also end with one vowel + one consonant, but the *first* syllable is stressed. The vowel in the final syllable has the 'schwa' sound:

★ <u>ga</u>llop   <u>op</u>en   <u>vis</u>it   <u>al</u>ter   <u>roc</u>ket   <u>bud</u>get

If the *final* syllable of the root word is the weak one, don't double the consonant, for example:

★ gallop + ed = galloped   open + ing = opening

Now add the suffix '-**ed**' to: visit   alter   rocket   budget

C | MIXED DOUBLES

Try some mixed practice. Copy and complete the following table. Remember the rule: *double the consonant only if the last syllable of the root word is the strong one, and you do not already have enough consonants to protect the short vowel sound.*

The first one of each has been done for you.

ROOT WORD	SUFFIXES	ROOT WORDS + SUFFIXES	
submit	-ing, -ed	submitting	_____
regret	-ing, -ed	regretting	_____
perform	-er, -ing	performer	_____
permit	-ing, -ed	permitting	_____
equip	-ed, -ment	equipped	_____
desert	-er, -ing	deserter	_____
blossom	-ing, -ed	blossoming	_____

Follow-on: Look back at your work and put the words that double in your Personal Spelling Dictionary.

> **Key point –** Listen for where the stressed syllable is when adding a vowel suffix to a word, to help you decide whether to double the consonant.

Units 38–42 cover spelling in context

Aim:
to help you speed up your dictionary skills

A   INCREASE YOUR SPEED

All professional writers use dictionaries. Even good spellers have to check some words. But perhaps you sometimes think: 'I won't bother looking it up because it will take me ages to find the word!'

With a little practice you can easily increase your speed. First, refresh your memory of alphabetical order. Write each set of words below in the correct alphabetical order:

1. monkey   gorilla   baboon   ape   chimpanzee   orangutan
2. swimming   skiing   snooker   soccer   sailing   shooting
3. John   James   Jonathan   Javed   Justin   Jeremy   Jack
4. Vicky   Kelly   Susan   Vera   Kim   Sarah   Katy   Vanessa
5. America   Antarctica   Australia   Africa   Angola   Austria

A Now take any dictionary. Estimate where the middle is and open it there. You will probably find that you have opened it at words beginning with 'M' – or very near to 'M'.

B Estimate where the middle of each half is. Compare with someone else to see if you arrive at the same letters.

E–L   M–R
A–D   S–Z

All dictionaries are slightly different. Some may have extra pages as part of the introduction and some may have a large appendix. Many dictionaries divide as shown here.

To remember the first letter of each quarter-section of the dictionary, make up a mnemonic, for example:

Andy **E**ats **M**armite **S**andwiches *or*
All **E**lephants **M**ake **S**quirts

C Work with a partner. Take it in turns to name any letter and see how many times your partner can open the dictionary at exactly that letter. Keep a record of your scores.

B | USE THE GUIDE WORDS

Most dictionaries have guide words at the top of each page. The guide word on the left gives you the first word on that page and the guide word on the right gives you the last word:

kilometre   **kipper**

of weight [F. f. Gk. *khilioi* thousand]

kilometre *n.* a metric measurement of distance equal to 1000 metres [Gk. *metron* measure]

kiloton *n.* a unit of explosive power equal

children of pre-school age [Ger. garden]

kind-hearted *adj.* of a kind and generous nature [OE *gecynd*e kind, *heorte* heart]

kindle *v.* **1.** to set on fire. **2.** to catch fire or burst into flame. **3.** to arouse emotion

Guide words save time. Look at the two guide words to work out if your word will be on that page.

Imagine these are the guide words at the tops of various pages.

p. 63: **brain   bread**
p. 465: **mountain   mumble**
p. 732: **splash   split**

p. 138: **duchess   dummy**
p. 466: **mummy   music**
p. 733: **splosh   sponge**

Based on the words and pages above, write the following words and estimate the number of the page where you would find each one. (The first one is done for you.)

★ duckling – p. 138   brave   spoil   museum
   mouth   splendid   multiply

Follow-on: Work in pairs and challenge each other to find different words in set times. Keep a record of your times, and compare your three best results.

> **Key point –** Learn to use your dictionary efficiently. It is a great spelling aid.

39 Computer spell-checks

Aim:
to find out when a computer spell-check program can help you – and when it can't

A | WHAT CAN SPELL-CHECK PROGRAMS DO?

Most modern computers have a spell-check on their word-processing program. Below is a typical spell-check program. When you open the spell-checker the spell-check window will appear, and your mistakes will be highlighted on the screen. It will ask you if you want to change anything.

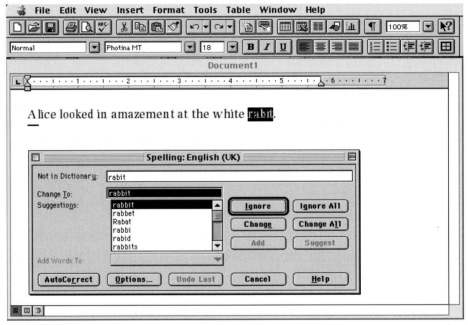

You have several options:

1 Perhaps you can see your mistake. If so type it in correctly and click on '**Change**'.

2 If you are not sure how to spell the word, click on '**Suggest**'. The computer will search its own dictionary and try to match the word with those like it. It might give you several words to choose from. Double-click on the one that looks right and the computer will replace your spelling.

3 Sometimes you might type a special name which the computer does not have in its dictionary. If it says the spelling is incorrect, you can tell it to '**Ignore**' that spelling.

4 If the special name is one that you will want to use again, you can tell the computer to '**Add**' it to its memory. Then it won't keep trying to check that word.

Type this sentence *exactly* as it is here, then run your spell-check program to correct all the mistakes.

★ I am typeing this sentense with meny delibrat speling mistaks to see how the spell-chek program werks on this computter.

B | BEAT THE COMPUTER

You may think your computer spell-check is brilliant, but it is still not as clever as your own brain! Check this out by typing in these sentences *exactly* as they are here:

★ I wonder weather this computer will fined all my mistaks. How dose it no witch words are rong? Has it mist any words?

Now run the spell-check. Your computer will probably spot only two words: **mistaks** and **rong**. There are six other mistakes.

Why did the computer miss the other mistakes? Can you correct them yourself?

C | CAN YOUR COMPUTER COPE WITH PROPER NOUNS?

All spell-check programs will be able to cope with well-known proper nouns such as days of the week and months. Some programs will also have the most common names of people and places stored in memory, for example:

★ London   Liverpool   Australia   James   Sarah   Jones

Try typing some of these proper nouns and see if the spell-check knows them. Type:

1 Your name and the names of some of your friends or family.
2 Places you have visited on holiday or places you would like to visit.
3 Your favourite football teams or pop stars.

Use the 'Add' command to add some proper nouns to the spell-check memory.

4 Does it recognise all the words in your school address? If not, add them.
5 Add any other proper nouns you think would be useful to future users.

> **Key point** – Computer spell-checks are a great help, as long as you are aware of the pitfalls.

Aim:
to find out why English spelling can be hard

A | THE HISTORY OF ENGLISH WORDS

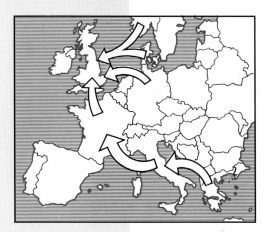

Have you ever wondered *why* English spelling has so many difficult words? Many languages always use the same letters for each sound. English has several choices for some sounds. This is because the language comes from not just one country, but from the many different peoples who have invaded or settled here in the past 2000 years.

Look at this table to see how some of our modern words originated:

OLD LANGUAGE	OLD WORD	OLD MEANING	MODERN WORD
Old English (Anglo-Saxon)	wealcan	roll about	walk
Old Norse (Viking)	steik	roast on a spit	steak
French	jeter	throw	jet
Latin	villa	house	village
Latin	gladius	sword	gladiator
Greek	hora	hour	hour

Some dictionaries tell us the origins of words, for example:

★ **guzzle** – eat or drink greedily. [OF *gosiller* chatter, vomit f. *gosier* throat]
★ **volcano** – mountain with an opening through which lava and gases are expelled. [L *Volcanus* Vulcan, Roman God of Fire]

Dictionaries normally indicate the original languages in brackets. Sometimes a word has passed through several languages on its way to English. This is shown by 'f.' for 'from':

★ **comet** – ball of ice , dust and gas, with long tail, orbiting in space. [ME f. OF *comete* f. L cometa f. Gk *kometes* long-haired]

Match up the abbreviations with the full words:

OE	F	L	f
Gk	ME	OF	ON

Old French	Greek	Middle English
Old Norse (Viking)		Old English (Anglo-Saxon)
Latin	from	French

B | GUESS THE MODERN WORD

Over the years, words often change to mean different things. The word 'gymnastics' comes from the Greek word *gumnos* meaning naked. In ancient times athletes trained naked so the word *gumnazo* came to mean 'train, practise'.

Complete this table. Read the information about the origin of each word and guess the modern word.

OLD WORDS	OLD MEANING	CLUE	NEW WORD
Gk geo + Gk graphe	earth + writing	school subject	
L computare	count up, reckon	electronic machine	
OE waecce	awake	worn on the wrist	
ON happ	luck	glad, cheerful	
OE plega	exercise	fun, amusement	
L carta	paper	funny drawing or film	

People all over the world now communicate and trade with one another. New words with different spelling patterns to English enter our language every year, for example:

LANGUAGE	WORD	HOW ENGLISH WOULD SPELL IT
Japanese	karaoke	English uses 'c' with the vowel 'a' (e.g. 'cat')
Norwegian	ski	English words don't end in 'i'
Italian	cappucino	English uses 'ch' to spell /ch/

New inventions need new words. Sometimes these are made from the initial letters of other words. Work out these acronyms:

ⓐ Light Amplification by Stimulated Emission of Radiation = _____

ⓑ Radio Detection And Ranging = _____

> **Key point –** Knowing how English has developed from different languages can help you to remember the different spelling patterns – and the 'rule-breakers'.

41 American English: 'our' and 're'

Aim:
to study the way in which some words are spelt differently in the USA

A   A LETTER FROM AMERICA

Read this letter:

> Hi David,
>
> It was great to get your letter last week. So you are still slaving away at school? We started our vacation two weeks ago. Mom, Dad, brother Bud and I headed straight for Florida where our neighbors have a cabin by the Everglades. We plan to stay with them until Labor Day, which is near the end of August. Most of the time we have been savoring the delights of the open country or fishing at a small harbor about three kilometers from here.
>
> On Monday we heard a rumor that an open-air theater in the center of Orlando was to be the scene of a colorful procession depicting thirteenth-century knights in armor. We clamored to be allowed to go and Dad eventually agreed. It was well worth it to see the splendor as the knights played out acts of valor. Unfortunately, little Bud, who is not much more than a meter tall, had a very poor view and started to complain. As he got more and more bored he started crawling around on the floor, untying the shoe laces of the onlookers. We endeavored to ignore his behavior but Dad was rapidly losing his sense of humor and we were dragged away before the show had ended!
>
> We are all looking forward to hearing news of your vacation (sorry – I should say holiday) so do write soon.
>
>   Good wishes from
>   your cousin Clark

B   LANGUAGE AND SPELLING DIFFERENCES

'American English' sometimes uses different words from ours. Clark obviously knows that what he calls a 'vacation' is a 'holiday' to us. Copy the table opposite and complete the gaps. Work in small groups to discuss ideas.

UK WORD	USA WORD
petrol	
pavement	
	trunk (of a car)
wardrobe	
	flashlight
	garbage
football	

Some spellings are also different in the USA. Look again at Clark's letter.

1 Find the word **colorful**.

We spell **colour** with the ending '**our**'. They spell it with '**or**'.

The Americans have made the same changes to all the English '**our**' words of more than one syllable. Words of one syllable, like **our**, **your**, and **flour** stay the same.

2 Find the word **center**.

We spell it **centre**. This is because the word came from Old French.

The Americans have changed all the '**re**' endings to '**er**'. This makes them easier to spell, because the letters '**er**' usually make the sound /er/ as in **letter**, **sister**, **driver**.

How many examples of both spelling changes can you find in Clark's letter? Write them all down in a table with two headings – one for USA spellings and one for UK spellings.

You should have a total of 13 '**our**' words and four '**re**' words.

Follow-on: Discuss with a friend why you think the Americans have made the changes they have.

Key point – Be alert to different ways of spelling the same word, and use the right one for the country you are in!

42 Brand names – deliberate misspells

Aim:
to look at some deliberately wrong spellings

A SPOT THE MISTAKE

People who want to advertise a product, a shop or a business often use the wrong spelling deliberately. Why do you think they do this? Discuss your ideas.

Copy the names from the advertisements here, then put the correct spellings beside them.

Now try these. The clue tells you what type of product or shop is being advertised. Write down both spellings.

1. Klive's Kamera Kabin (*photography shop*)
2. Whiskas (*cat food*)
3. Prop-U-Up (*pillow*)
4. Krumbs Tea Room (*café*)
5. Kall Kwik (*printer*)
6. Odor Eaters (*insole for trainer shoes*)
7. Irn-Bru (*drink*)
8. K'Nex (*construction toy*)
9. Sydewynder (*skateboard*)

B AMATEUR ADVERTISER

Imagine it is your job to advertise these products or businesses. Attract the attention of the public by making up a new way of spelling the words – but remember that the word you write must sound the same, or nearly the same, as the original.

1. Chocolate creams (*biscuits*)
2. Copper-bright (*metal polish*)
3. Bert's Burgers (*burger bar*)
4. Buildings bricks (*children's toy*)
5. Space Speeder (*arcade game*)
6. Quality Shoes (*shoe shop*)

Compare your work with a friend's. Which words would attract most attention?

C | SHOP NAMES WITH HOMOPHONES

Instead of deliberately spelling words wrongly, some firms attract attention by using homophones. These are also called 'puns', or a 'play on words':

Pete's Plaice   Dress Cents   Paws Here   Hairport   Suite Dreams

Write the name of each shop, and beside it write the other spelling for the odd word.

Now try these. The clue tells you what type of shop or firm is being advertised. Write down both spellings.

1. Hair We Are (*hairdresser*)
2. Meet Here (*butcher*)
3. Toad on the Road (*breakdown trucks*)
4. Best Cellars (*wine shop*)
5. His 'n' Hairs (*hairdresser*)

Follow-on: Some people (especially some teachers!) complain about advertisements which use the wrong spelling. They say it will confuse people and encourage bad spelling. Is it going to *confuse* your spelling to look for and collect odd spellings – or do you think it could even be a *help*? Discuss this in groups and give your reasons.

> **Key point –** It can be fun to spot odd spellings and puns – but take care not to use these in the wrong place!

COPYMASTER 42

Section 2: Self-assessment page

Complete this page to see how much you have learnt.

A | SPELLING PATTERNS

Write out the incomplete words, choosing the correct letters to fill the gaps.

1. ___onest, Miss, I was lis___ing so I don't ___now how I got the ___rong ans___.
2. The dawn of a new ___tury was ___ebrated all around the w___ld.
3. After considering the matter th___ly, Karen made her dec___.
4. His teenage ambi___ was to be a rock musi___ rather than a politi___.
5. Despite the prese___ of a fero___ g___rd dog, a qu___tity of anti___ were stolen.
6. When the en___ cau___ fire, the ch___f me___anic sounded the emer___ siren.

B | HOMOPHONES

A computer could not correct these mistakes because they are real words but used in the wrong context. Write out each phrase, changing the incorrect word.

1. a short paws
2. bird of pray
3. join the cue
4. the mane reason
5. have a brake
6. board and fed up
7. read allowed
8. heavy-wait

C | WEAK VOWELS

One vowel is missing from some of the words below. Each one has the neutral 'schwa' sound, so listening will not help you. You must think how the word looks. Write the words with the correct vowel.

1. a desper___te situation
2. a scarcely aud___ble sound
3. a film direct___r
4. defin___tely my favour___te
5. a spectacul___r display
6. an advis___ble move

D | SUFFIXES

Think about the suffix rules and write this passage, correcting the words in italics.

For *centurys* scientists have been *commited* to *solveing* problems for the purpose of *benefitting* mankind. In *earlyer* days they had little *equippment* but still made many *amazeing discoverys*. When *factorys* first *openned*, *safty* was not a major concern but, as people became more *qualified*, a more *careing* environment *developed*. These days *supplyes* of *servicable* goods are *plentyful* and the old days of dangerous working conditions are *easyly forgoten*.

/ / – when you see these two lines it means that the letters between them tell you what sound to say. Many dictionaries use this symbol to tell readers how to pronounce new words. The last word in the 's' section of some dictionaries is '*syzygy*'. Most dictionaries would include a phonic (or sound) code for this, which might be: /sĭzĭjĭ/.

Breve – the code used by some dictionaries to show a short vowel sound. A breve is a small curly mark above the vowel.
Examples: /ă/ as in **add**, /ĕ/ as in **egg**, /ĭ/ as in **ill**, /ŏ/ as in **odd**, /ŭ/ as in **up**.

Consonants – the letters **b c d f g h j k l m n p q r s t v w x y z**. Consonants don't make any sense on their own. They need to be with vowels to make a word or a syllable. The word 'consonant' comes from the Latin words *con* meaning 'with' and *sonant* meaning 'sound'.

Cursive writing – joined-up writing. If you practise words in cursive writing the letters flow smoothly together, and your hand somehow helps your brain to remember the spelling.

Homophones – words which sound the same but have different meanings and different spellings.
Examples: **road/rode**, **flower/flour**, **nose/knows**.
The word 'homophone' comes from two Greek words: *homos* meaning 'same' and *phone* meaning 'sound'.

Macron – the code used by some dictionaries to show a long vowel sound. A macron is a straight line above the vowel.
Examples: /ā/ as in **alien**, /ē/ as in **emu**, /ī/ as in **island**, /ō/ as in **over**, /ū/ as in **universe**.

Mnemonic – (*pronounced 'nemonic' – the 'm' is silent*) a memory aid. It could be a picture, a verse, a sentence – anything which jogs your memory.
Example: to remember how to spell 'necessary' you could think:
'It is ne**c**e**ss**ary to have one **c**ollar and **two s**ocks', or
'**N**ever **e**at **c**hips, **e**at **s**ausage **s**andwiches **a**nd **r**aspberry **y**oghurt'.
The word 'mnemonic' comes from a Greek word *mnemon* meaning 'mindful'.

Prefix – the letters added to the start of a word to change its meaning.
Examples: **dis** + agree, **un** + do, **mis** + print, **re** + build, **super** + sonic.

Schwa – the word used to describe a weak or a 'neutral' vowel sound. This sound is found in some *unstressed* syllables. A syllable with a 'schwa' sound can be hard to spell because there is no clear vowel sound to give you a clue. It is similar to /ŭ/ or /er/ but can be spelt in many different ways. Some dictionaries use this code to show the 'schwa' sound: /ə/.
Examples: mountain /**mountən**/, compare /**cəmpare**/, hospital /**hospitəl**/.
The word 'schwa' comes from a Hebrew word meaning 'emptiness'.

Study, **Cover**, **Write**, **Check** – the 'golden rule' of learning to spell well. If you just copy a word, you may not remember it. It's far better to learn new words by looking at them carefully, and then writing them from memory.

Suffix – a letter or letters added to the end of a word to change its meaning.
Examples: amaze + **s** = **amazes**;   + **ed** = **amazed**;   + **ing** = **amazing**;
+ **ment** = **amazement**.
Adding suffixes can lead to spelling problems because sometimes you need to change the root word. To help with these rules, we divide suffixes into two types:
Vowel suffixes – those which start with a vowel, for example:
-ed -ing -er -est -y -ous -able
Consonant suffixes – those which start with a consonant, for example:
-ful -ly -ness -ment

Syllables – the 'beats' in a word.
Examples: **in** has one syllable; **inside** has two syllables; **inbetween** has three syllables; **intelligent** has four syllables; **individual** has five syllables. Each syllable has one vowel sound. In words of more than one syllable, one of the syllables has a stronger sound than the rest. We call this one the *stressed* syllable.
Examples: **mountain   beware   monster   fantastic   important**.

Vowels – the letters **a e i o u**. Vowels are like the filling in a sandwich – every word must contain at least one vowel. Longer words must have a vowel sound in every syllable. The letter '**y**' can also count as a vowel when it has the sound /ē/ as in 'silly' or /ī/ as in 'fly'.
Long vowels – these have the same sound as the letters' names.
Examples: **ālien, ēqual, īce, ōld, ūse**.
Short vowels – you probably learnt these sounds when you first started school.
Examples: **ănt, ĕngine, ĭgloo, ŏctopus, ŭpset**.
Vowel digraphs – two letters used together to make one vowel sound.

Examples:				
ar – artist	**er** – driver	**ir** – shirt	**or** – short	**ur** – nurse
ai – train	**ay** – pray	**ee** – team	**ea** – beat	**oa** – toad
oo – room	**oy** – boy	**oi** – boil	**ew** – new	
ow – snow, cow	**ou** – cloud, young, soup	**ie** – chief, pie		